MAGI FROM THE EAST

HOW THE WISE MEN CHALLENGE CHRISTIANITY'S APPROACH TO ASTROLOGY

JANELLE LARA

CONTENTS

Foreword ix
By Rachel Olstad, M.A.

Preface xiii

1. Framing the Search for Truth 1
2. An Exegesis of Matthew 2:1-12 and its Historical Context 20
3. Who Were the Magi, and What was the Star? 36
4. Astrology 49
   Pagan Practice or the 'report that goes forth throughout all the earth?'
5. What Would Jesus Do? 71
6. "Everything is Demonic" 83
   A Commentary on the Cultural Response to Spirituality within the Church
7. What is the Point? 97
8. (Bonus) Astrology Basics 109

Additional Resources: 121

"Whatever things were rightly said among all men, are the property of us Christians." -Justin Martyr
(*Second Apology, Chapter 13*)

To my husband, Robert- thank you for believing in me and for your endless love and support.

To my precious children- it is an honor to raise you, and to love you.

To all Mothers who wish their kids came with an instruction manual- they did. Here is your permission to use it.

FOREWORD

BY RACHEL OLSTAD, M.A.

If you are reading this, you are probably not very different from me. I wear a lot of hats, and I'm deeply passionate about all of them. I am a wife, a mom of three, and my life is guided by faith, family and a serious commitment to being a life-long learner. I'm a language lover (bilingual in English and French) and I've spent over a decade in various roles within the realm of education. Like Janelle, I was born and raised Catholic, and faith is the foundation of my life.

When I talk about my faith, the pursuit of knowledge, and the search for truth—I don't speak lightly. This may sound a bit cliché, but my favorite Bible verse since I was a young girl has been Proverbs 3:5-6: "Trust in the LORD with all your heart, and do not lean on your own understanding. In all your ways acknowledge him, and he will make straight your paths."

For years, I believed "not leaning on my own understanding" meant sticking strictly to what I was taught and told…but deep down I've always been a questioner—someone who struggles to follow a rule unless I truly understand the depth of its *why*. My nature is to dive deep, uncover meaning, and challenge the surface of any topic, which is probably why I've always been drawn to the complexities of faith and life.

Like most people, my first encounter with astrology was the generic horoscope section—the fluffy, fake, pop culture nonsense you find in a newspaper or a magazine. Honestly? It fell completely flat. It felt fake, forced, and ridiculous. It didn't have any substance, and it felt like a random guessing game. It certainly wasn't the kind of deep, meaningful truth I crave—let alone anything I thought could be related to God.

Everything changed in 2020 when I was re-introduced to astrology through Janelle. What she shared and taught me through her own studies and research wasn't some fortune-telling gimmick; it was a profound spiritual framework. The revelation for me was slow and often painful as I grappled with the potential that these "occult/new age" studies could be filled with darkness. I feared they would lead me astray from my faith.

I was wrong. The more I doubled down on my own research (with lots of prayer and caution) I came to learn, know and believe something different; that astrology could in fact be another connection point with God - from God. The logic is simple and profound: God made the earth, stars, and planets, and God made us. So couldn't the stars also be one of the many ways He acknowledges us and guides our paths? God created everything good, and His truth cannot contradict itself.

My previous "understanding"—which was simply judgment and fear in disguise—was challenged, and I realized that fully trusting God didn't mean avoiding difficult questions—it meant diving into them with faith as my guide. I now view and use astrology not as a scary occult practice, but as a "language of God." As a student of languages, I love thinking about how the stars can communicate with us and point us in the right direction, both literally and figuratively.

Through the study of astrology in this light-filled approach, I've gained wisdom and practical insights that have profoundly deepened every relationship in my life. It has helped me better see and love myself, my husband, my children, my parents, friends, and colleagues. And here is the truly sacred part: my understanding of astrology didn't replace my love, faith, trust in God or Catholic faith—it deepened it in every way.

In these pages, Janelle wrestles with God and with long-held religious fears, bringing academic rigor and the Catholic intellectual tradition to a topic often filled with ignorance. She doesn't ask you to abandon your faith; she asks you to expand your understanding of a God who is infinitely loving and generous with His means of communication.

Whether you're already on the pathway to discovering the power of astrology, or you're a person of faith like me who is still struggling with this topic, Janelle's work is a must-read. This book is a courageous step toward understanding the fullness of the truth God has already revealed.

My hope for you, the reader, is simple: that through this groundbreaking work, you will find the same peace and assurance that the universe, the stars, the planets, and the cosmos—as God created it—can offer guidance, self-acceptance, and a beautiful, useful map for your life and your faith.

So, I urge you: open your mind and your heart, and see what God has in store for you through this work, starting with the beautiful story of the Magi.

PREFACE

In his 1946 work *Man's Search for Meaning*, Viktor Frankl details his harrowing experiences in various concentration camps during World War II. Frankl—who was a young husband and a brilliant psychologist—would lose all of his family in the concentration camps, including his pregnant wife. Trapped in horrific living conditions and unsure if he would ever make it out alive, Frankl resolved that if he did live, he would one day share the experiences of genocide and the horrors of the Nazi death camps through the eyes of a trained psychologist with the world. This mission gave him a reason to live. It gave his suffering meaning, which became critical to his survival. Frankl became not only a victim of great brutality, but also an observer. Amidst cold, hunger, and exposure, he would scribble notes of his experiences on scraps of paper that he hid in his pockets—hoping to remember important details if and when he was given the opportunity to share them.

After his liberation, Frankl used his insights to teach millions of readers worldwide that human beings are uniquely equipped not only to survive terrible events but also to transform hardship into meaning—a crucial aspect of human flourishing.

As one can imagine, this experience extended well to Frankl's return to working with mental health patients. "Mental Health is based on a certain degree of tension, the tension between what one has already achieved and what one still ought to accomplish, or the gap between what one is and what one should become." He notes that those who were the most likely to survive the Nazi concentration camps were those like him, "those who knew that there was a task waiting for them to fulfill."[1] Huh. Not those who had the most to go home to, not those who were the most moral or religious, not even the healthiest or the youngest (though I'm sure youth and vigor certainly helped)— but the ones who had a larger purpose to fulfill. It was those who were acutely aware of that for which they were created, those who had some knowledge of the mission endowed to them by their creator, who survived one of the darkest moments in history.

This stands in stark contrast to the 'dream' that is being promoted on every street corner and billboard in America. The idea that the meaning of life is to 'self-actualize', to achieve success, to make money and to collect items, to travel the world… until finally—one retires on some golf course somewhere, after having enjoyed a lifetime of self-aggrandizement and comfort has permeated every corner of our Great Nation. Many would argue that devotion to this philosophy has weakened our character.

Frankl's riveting account challenges this notion, and pushes

---

1. Frankl, Viktor E. 2015. *Man's Search for Meaning*. Beacon Press, 104-105.

one to wonder—what if the good life is not one free from all tension, and safe from all discomfort? What if it is one where we are intimately aware of the mission placed in front of us? One where we are aware of our strengths and weaknesses, and one where we have a mind bent and heart directed toward the Creator who assigned this mission to us? Hopefully, this 'certainty of mission' does not necessitate a hardship so great as surviving a concentration camp. But don't we all, deep down have a desire to overcome *something*? Even the Churches don't teach this often enough, to the great spiritual peril and mental boredom of their members.

Every single human being has been created with a task that is urgent for them to fulfill.[2] In the Bible, which is God's self-revelation to human beings, God begins by sharing something very important about himself, right from the start. He is a creator, and all that God creates is good. As renowned Psychologist Jordan B. Peterson emphasizes at length in his book *We Who Wrestle with God*—it is God himself who creates order out of chaos. In his observations of the creation story in Genesis, Peterson notes, "the biblical account ascribes to each of us a value that places us at the very pinnacle of creation."[3] Starting with the heavens and the earth, and ascending in value to the vegetation upon the earth, to the animals, and finally to human beings—it is very obvious in the creation story that everything created in the heavens and on the earth was created for human beings, who were created for God.

---

2. "Before I formed you in the womb I knew you, before you were born I dedicated you, a prophet to the nations I appointed you." Jeremiah 1:5
3. Peterson, Jordan B. 2024. *We Who Wrestle with God: Perceptions of the Divine*. Portfolio, 3-5.

PREFACE

"The Lord has made everything for a purpose" (Proverbs 16:4).

What then, could be the purpose of the planets, the stars in the sky, and the constellations? Well, He tells us. "And God said, 'Let there be lights in the dome of the sky to separate the day from the night; and let them be for signs, and for seasons, and for days and years.'"[4] The heavens are clearly meant to communicate with us- not only for time but also for signs. Allegedly, there is also a silent "report that goes forth through all the Earth." (Psalm 19:2-5) What could this report look like, literally speaking?

The book that you have in your hands is both a personal anthology and an academic exploration of these questions. In seeking to understand the purpose of the heavens, I consider the various and complex ways God communicates with humankind. Could ancient peoples, seeking the same existential meaning Victor Frankl clung to so desperately in Auschwitz, have discovered a cosmological language so complex that it took thousands of years to discern? Could astrology be an insight into the mind of God? Or is it a wholly pagan practice—devoid of true spiritual meaning and replete with psychological phenomena like the Barnum Effect, which explains why it sometimes works?[5]

There are several reasons why I consider answering these questions a worthwhile endeavor, not least because interest in astrology has heightened in recent years. Another motivation can be described thus: it is the opinion of the

---

4. Genesis 1:14 (NRSV)
5. The Barnum Effect: The idea that people tend to accept very vague, general statements as highly personal and accurate — especially if they're flattering. Psychics, horoscopes, and personality quizzes often rely heavily on this.

author that the time has come for God's people to return to an understanding of ancient wisdom and traditional knowledge—up to and including the study and interpretation of the cosmos. At risk of sounding existential—the time is nigh, and the calling feels urgent.

Tragic are the generations past who spurned ancestral wisdom, convinced they knew best.[6]

Ad Majorem Dei Gloriam,
Janelle Lara

---

[6]. "'Then one of the priests, a very old man, said: "Solon, Solon, you Greeks never grow up. There isn't an old man among you." "What do you mean?" Solon replied. "None of you have mature minds," the priest replied. "You have no ancient tradition to imbue your minds with old beliefs and with understanding aged by time. The reason for this is that the human race has often been destroyed in various ways– as it will be in the future too." Plato, Robin Waterfield, and Andrew Gregory. 2008. *Timaeus and Critias*. Oxford University Press, 9.

1
FRAMING THE SEARCH FOR TRUTH

Growing up, I was the model Catholic girl.

As the typical eldest daughter from an immigrant family, I took very seriously the stories my parents told me about how siblings often follow in the footsteps of the oldest.

"There was a girl I knew who lived in my neighborhood growing up", one of my parents would begin, "and one day, she got in with the wrong crowd, started doing drugs and drinking, and ruined her whole life. Then one by one, every single one of her siblings followed suit. The choices you make will be very important not only for your life—but for your brothers and sister too."

I listened with wide-eyes, taking in everything they told me. I'm not sure if the stories are true—but my parents did a great job driving home the idea that the decisions you make (especially during the early years of your life) have an impact larger than you can imagine. At a young age, (and by the grace of God) I decided to attempt to make exclusively good decisions.

I started with religion. I fully committed to my faith in a way that many Catholic School kids don't. I was an altar server, attended youth group, and even though I had a stint when I was not making *the best* choices in boys, I remained a virgin until marriage. At age nineteen, after attending college and seeing first—hand the pain that casual relationships and hook-up culture caused, I wrote a book. "Confessions of a Pure Heart" which was an immature albeit heartwarming teenage attempt at influencing my peers for good. While completing my bachelors and masters degrees, I would spend my early twenties giving talks in local churches, preaching abstinence and selling the books at a table afterwards.

However, underneath this veneer lied a deeply sad heart. Through a series of unfortunate events that happened when I was a small child, I grew up with something that my therapist would later identify as, "Relational Trauma". But I didn't know what that was until my mid-thirties. So I spent my teenage and young adult years having almost nightly anxiety attacks, performing for love (think every honor society and accolade you can imagine), and waiting for the day when I could fulfill my dream of creating my own family—one free from conflict and heartache.

These panic attacks would last until I married my husband, which is still the best decision I've ever made. "*Finally*" I thought. <u>Finally</u> I could fulfill the dream I'd had since I was a little girl. All I had ever wanted was to be barefoot in the garden with my perfect children, blissfully grateful for my husband. We would have the perfect home (complete with a white picket fence) filled with love and laughter. Finally, I could leave the sadness behind.

This plan would have worked out great, except we live in the real world. Even though my husband and I *wanted* the same things, we both came from high-conflict immigrant families who thought therapy was for crazy people. As much as we tried to create a healthier relationship than those we had observed when we were young, we often fell back into old patterns. The result was that we argued often —too often. As soon as our honeymoon, I realized that this blissful dream of a perfect family was fading away.

But, we were from a new generation. We knew we needed therapy. We were determined to create the marriage we both wanted, and that determination only grew with the birth of the child conceived just two months after our wedding day. Our daughter solidified our resolve. We were not going to repeat the patterns with which we were raised —we were going to give her something better.

Cue the kitchen sink. We did couples therapy, went on marriage retreats, did spiritual direction together… you name it. We prayed together, listened to podcasts, read books together, and wrote each other letters. We tried having more sex and we tried abstaining from sex, we did date nights and we prioritized family time… we picked up hobbies, tried new conversational techniques ("So before I respond, what I'm hearing is") … you get the picture.

While much of what we learned was helpful, it was also exhausting. Despite our best efforts, we persisted in creating the high-conflict relationship that we had been trying so hard to avoid. Like so many others, we felt doomed to repeat the unhealthy patterns we grew up with.

Then, everything changed.

I will never forget New Years 2020. A devastating family tragedy would happen that day, which I would not find out about until eighteen months later. As far as I could tell, it was a normal New Years, aside from the increased excitement about entering a new decade. "The Roaring Twenties" people said, anticipating life would only get better and better (much like the original twenties), as people often do during a bull market. My husband and I left our daughter with my parents and went out on the town, excited to have some fun together.

However, the frustrations in our marriage continued— despite our best efforts. Just a short time before, I had started getting sick and tired of arguing. Our relationship echoed a hurt I had felt my entire life, "You say that you love me, but you don't even *know* me". When I got married, I thought I had found my person, the one who would love all of me, even the parts I didn't know how to love myself. The constant arguing and lack of understanding created an "Et tu, Brute?" moment for me. (And, I am sure my husband felt the same, and experienced a similar betrayal from me) *Even you won't love me? Even you can only handle me if I hide my favorite parts of me?* I had been an imaginative, smart, energetic and fast-talking child… but that was not what the world wanted. I had spent my life shrinking, being perfectly obedient, over-explaining, and attempting to become more palatable for those around me. I kept waiting, expecting, hoping someone would love me enough to look at me and say, "What are you doing Janelle?! No no no, stop this. You are brilliant. You are beautiful. You are meant to shine." But alas, my fictional Italian grandmother never came. So, like many others I continued people-pleasing, denying myself, and submitting to those who were all too happy to take advantage of my emaciated spiritual state (and of course, erupting in anger periodically as a result of my self-betrayal).[1]

This means that by the end of 2019, I had said the word "divorce" to my husband for the very first time. While I was failing miserably at the relationship I most wanted to succeed at—I had managed to ride the Consulting Boom of the late twenty-teens and built an online business that allowed me to shine and be seen in all of the ways I wasn't at home. My marketing and consulting company was making multiple six-figures, and I was able to work just twenty hours a week and stay home with my daughter while my husband was in school. Like many working women who make more than their husbands, I wondered what on earth I needed him for.

However, I was a deeply religious woman, and I knew the damage that children experience when they grow up without their fathers. Despite what I had gone through as a child, I am grateful my parents did what they could to stay together. I knew that the devil hates marriage, he hates family, and that it was him who wanted us to divorce.

My husband knew it too, which is why—after a few drinks to loosen up his emotions—he poured his heart out to me in a rare moment of vulnerability while I drove us home from our New Years festivities. "How could you want to divorce me?" he said through tears, "I love you." My heart broke.

The truth is, I loved him too (and still love him, deeply). He

---

[1]. I am not alone in this, most of us walk around this way— and we continue to do so until we are taught how to *actually* love ourselves, with a Christ-like love. It is a lesson many never learn.

is an exceptional person and an amazing Dad. Despite our different attachment styles and ways of communicating, he has always been my very best friend. He did more at home and spent more time with our daughter than most men. Even though I had said the d-word, I didn't mean it. I couldn't go on the way things were, but I wasn't ready to give up. I just knew something had to change.

Coincidentally, right around this same time a podcast popped up in my feed. The words "Astrological Forecast 2020" appeared on my phone during the early days of January. I drew a quick breath when I saw it. A podcast that tended to lean more spiritual but also spoke about businesses had interviewed an Astrologer. But I was a Good Catholic Girl, remember? I had been taught that Astrology was demonic. I quickly deleted the podcast.

However, it didn't leave my mind. *"What even is astrology?"* I wondered. From the little I knew about it, it told people about themselves. Like most, I knew I was a Gemini, but not much else. I also knew that people tried to use it to make predictions, which is why it was sinful. I tried to push it out of my mind—but I was so frustrated with the way things were, that I couldn't keep myself from wondering if astrology had some knowledge that could help me. I wondered if there were any nuggets of wisdom that could give me a clue about why I was trying so hard in my marriage, with finances (which we had no clue how to manage), and with my weight (which ballooned as soon as I got pregnant) without success. After thinking about it for several days, I felt like I had to try. Out of desperation, and with a prayer to God to forgive me if it was wrong, I decided to listen to the podcast.

It was a forecast, and knowing what I know now, astrology is famously bad at making predictions (on top of the fact that "attempting to gain control over knowledge of the future"[2] is strictly forbidden, for good reason). BUT I was deeply impressed with how the Astrologer was able to speak the language of astrology and share her knowledge in a way that almost told a story... as if the planets were characters in a play that reflected the happenings here upon the earth. She didn't get too specific. For some reason, I felt safe with her. Going by my gut instinct alone, I recognized a strand of truth and decided to book an introductory call.

Soon, it became clear why I had been drawn to her. She was the maternal Italian figure I was looking for. Growing up Catholic in the Northeast, her Mom had always sought out astrologers. She was raised during the spiritual revolution of the 70s and 80s, but had also spent many years working in finance. Despite the esoteric subject matter, she had a groundedness that made me trust her—alongside a Boston accent and no-nonsense honesty that I loved.

I wanted to book a natal astrology session with her, and immediately thought about whether my husband would approve. I was going against what we'd both been taught—and doubted he would be on board. However, the feeling that there was something there that I needed to hear was unmistakable. While I was afraid of his response, I knew I needed to be honest.

I found him in the kitchen, cleaning up after dinner. "I don't want to tell you, which means I have to tell you" I

---

2. Ratzinger, Joseph Cardinal. 1995. *Catechism of the Catholic Church.* Image, Doubleday, 2116.

said in a quiet voice. "I don't know why, but I'm feeling pulled to have an appointment with that astrologer that I met… it doesn't feel wrong, like I might expect it to… I'm just scared of getting sucked into something evil." I held my breath, waiting for his response.

He responded with so much Christ-like love. "I trust you" he said, "And I trust God. It's ok to ask questions. If it's true, you will know, and if it's not true, you will know." I let out a sigh of relief and gave him a hug. "Thank you" I whispered. With his blessing, I scheduled the meeting.

THE REST IS HISTORY

That first astrology reading changed my life. It's hard to put into words, but I was no longer the same person afterwards (in ways that made it definitively clear that this was not the work of the devil). First, I experienced an intimacy with God that I had never been able to imagine, despite years going to Church every Sunday, praying rosaries, and being as good as I could possibly be (for the record, I still do all of those things, and advocate for them. They are the foundation of a good life). I could not believe how deeply God loves us, to create us on purpose and then to also be so kind as to give us a guide—a map of ourselves and one another. Finally, I understood why He made me the way he did. I realized that the qualities I often tried to hide or minimize are *precisely how* I fit into His larger mission. I also saw my vulnerabilities, the things I needed to watch out for, and the behavioral patterns that I should avoid all together.

I was also thrilled to discover that this guide was available *for every human being on the planet*. As spouses and parents, we always wish our people came with a guide—and I was so grateful to discover that they did! My husband and children's charts shed light on some of our differences, how each wanted to be loved, and the way each of them communicates. My chart gave me clarity on why I felt so disillusioned with the life we had created.

Of course, I don't credit all of the great things in my life to astrology. We can all have an amazing life without it. ("No one needs astrology, everyone needs Jesus" is a slogan I say regularly). But for me, the additional insights I gained of myself and those around me had a profound impact on my life and relationships. As my marriage steadily improved, I used the astrological insights that I gained about my family to love them as God made them.

Throughout this journey, I have recognized that my mission is that every single person will recognize that they are deeply seen, known and loved by the wonderful God who created them. He in his infinite goodness has provided you and those you love with a beautiful map with which to see, know and love you, too. Regardless of whether or not you choose to engage with astrology, I hope you encounter and come to love our awesome God.[3]

MY RESEARCH PHILOSOPHY

In my studies on ancient spiritual practices (specifically astrology) and their possible use by the Catholic faithful, I have been guided by an idea that Durham University Theologian Karen Kilby shared about St. Augustine of Hippo's theological method, "What Augustine quite

---

3. In every chapter, you will notice that I start with a more conversational tone as I share parts of my story. When I transition into my research, I will take on a more academic tone. This transition is intentional.

dramatically indicates is that the search for clarity, at its best, begins in confusion.. or rather, it begins an honesty about confusion, in the willingness to acknowledge what one does not understand, the willingness to consider and explore rather than suppress a difficulty, the willingness to articulate and examine a model rather than nervously push it under the carpet. " She continues, "and it is important to understand that what this in fact means is that the search for clarity begins in faith, in real conviction, in a very distinctive kind of confidence."[4] This 'confidence in faith while honestly acknowledging initial confusion' is a humble position that the Christian church culture in the United States of America often refuses to take. We focus so much on the fact that the Christian religion is the *correct* religion, that we don't acknowledge how much we still don't know (or quite possibly, how much we *forgot* during the ages of enlightenment, modernism, and post-modernism). We often refuse to be honest about the confusion that still exists, in particular when it comes to how we 'apply' theology to ever-changing cultural norms and societal struggles. Culturally, it seems that we have become so fixed on having an answer to every question that we forget to continue to expand the application of Christianity.

It is a distinct and important aspect of the Catholic Intellectual tradition that Christians are not only allowed, but encouraged to ask questions. According to our philosophical traditions that go back to Thomas Aquinas in the 1200s and beyond, faith simply *cannot* contradict reason—because God created both and the truth does not contradict itself. This means that as intellectuals, as human beings made in the image of God, and as Christians, we

---

4. Higton, Mike, and Jim Fodor. 2020. *The Routledge Companion to the Practice of Christian Theology (Routledge Religion Companions)*, 61.

have already been given confidence in the ultimate clarity —so we must not be afraid of pursuing difficult questions.

METHODS UTILIZED TO PROVE THE TRUTH OR FALSEHOOD OF ASTROLOGY

A critical aspect of 'doing theology' is acknowledging that right now we may not have a *full understanding* of the truth, even though it has already been *fully revealed* (and, that with this admission it does not automatically follow that we need to question the truth of the whole). In fact, because the truth has been revealed, it is up to us to go find it, if it is findable.[5] And when we do, we are to incorporate it into the Catholic Church, "the pillar and foundation of truth".[6]

As much as Christians may want to believe that ancient spirituality should be rejected altogether, science is beginning to disprove that assumption. Additionally, the Catholic Magisterium has not spoken definitively on the manner, other than to denounce attempting to tell the future or to gain control over the future and other people's lives.[7] Cognitive dissonance develops when practices lumped under "divination" begin to be used by hospitals nationwide, and this opens the door for inquiry into what other practices may have been falsely labeled.[8]

---

5. Aquinas acknowledges that there is some truth which is "philosophically unknowable", such as God's decision to love us. Kreeft, *Ethics for Beginners*, 126.
6. *NABRE - New American Bible Revised Edition*, 2010, Catholic Bible Publishers, 1 Timothy 3:15.
7. Ratzinger, Joseph Cardinal. 1995. *Catechism of the Catholic Church*. Image, Doubleday, 2115-2117.
8. An example is the practice of Reiki, which has been rejected categorically by the Catholic Church despite recent scientific evidence proving its efficacy, and its incorporation into hospitals nationwide. I've

It is with this 'open door' in mind that I pursue the truth of the modern-day Catholic and Christian Church's relationship with Astrology and other ancient spiritual traditions.

EXEGESIS

In the pursuit of the truth, my method begins with scripture. Evangelical Theologian Kevin J. Vanhoozer reminds us that "scripture is the 'soul of theology.'"[9] Indeed the scripture is designed to be a guide and to influence every aspect of our lives. Exegesis became an important method of my approach to this project. I rely extensively on the story of the Magi here.

Of course, there are challenges to relying on scripture:

> "Today, as throughout history, the temptation to use scripture to promote one's own theological agenda is great... the overarching purpose of scripture is not to serve as raw material for systems of theology but to serve as a charter and guide for the church and its performance as the body of Christ in the ongoing drama of redemption".[10]

Exegesis (meaning biblical study), while such an urgent priority, remains unhelpful if it is simply taking words out of context to promote your own belief systems. I am grateful for the work of Raymond Brown, David

---

written extensively about Reiki, including a paper which will be published in the journal 'Kaleidescope' in Spring 2026.
9. Higton, Mike, and Jim Fodor. 2020. *The Routledge Companion to the Practice of Christian Theology (Routledge Religion Companions)*, 141.
10. Higton, 157.

Harrington, and other giants in the study of scripture for offering the insights needed to make a less-biased analysis.

In order to ensure that I am not taking the Bible out of context, I conducted a critical historical analysis of the story of the Magi. Systematic Theologians like Joseph Ratzinger (also known as Pope Benedict the Sixteenth) and Ancient Languages/Religion Expert Roy Kotanski, both of whom approach the story with a scientific and historical lens, help guide my investigation. This is followed by a critical historical analysis of the origins and philosophy of Astrology itself.

Ultimately, the question I am answering is two-fold, 1. "Is Astrology the 'report that goes forth throughout all the earth'[11], or a demonic dupe?" and *if it is* the report God uses to communicate with us, 2. "How can Christians safely engage with this communication?' I believe the answer to these questions should go beyond a fear of the demonic (though that cannot be ruled out) and lands us within the graveyard of ancient wisdom which was lost during the 'Age of Enlightenment', Modernism and Post-Modernism.[12] Unfortunately, while Christians may not have gone so far as to claim that "God is dead", we have certainly embraced aspects of the cult of scientism, which essentially believes that if something cannot be measured or understood by what we already know, then it couldn't possibly exist. We maintain our religiosity by adding a twist, "or, it's demonic".

---

11. Psalm 19:2-5

12. I won't get into my thoughts on The Enlightenment era and how its ideologies often did more harm than good here, but I encourage readers to reference the book "Ethics for Beginners" by Peter Kreeft to get a better idea of how philosophy and ethics took a turn for the worst during this time.

To be clear, I am not saying we need to embrace every ancient or alternative spiritual practice with open arms. The result of inquiry into some practices may well be, "we need to avoid this altogether." The difference is that we need to ensure that we are speaking from a position of scientifically and/or philosophically accurate reasoning, not out of ignorance or fear. There but for the grace of God, go I.

As a result of my life experiences and my research, I have come to the conclusion that astrology is a language of God, created and used to communicate with his people, to mark the signs and seasons[13], and to support each individual in his or her mission in this life. To use astrology for specific predictions or to gain control over another is a wrong use of this gift, but it does not negate the practice altogether.

The biblical concept Jordan Peterson has made so popular, "wrestling with God" represents a very real and necessary aspect of our faith tradition. Along this vein, I am asking questions that push the fringes of Catholic belief with the goal of discerning the truth.

I take the discernment of truth very seriously. Pope Saint John Paul II echoed Aquinas when he said, "Religious faith itself calls for intellectual inquiry; and the confidence that there can be no contradiction between faith and reason is a distinctive feature of the Catholic humanistic tradition as it has existed in the past and as it exists in our own day."[14] Oxford-educated Catholic Priest Fr. Dwight Longenecker states the following after coming to his own conclusion

---

13. Genesis 1:14-19 and Job 38:32, NABRE.
14. Quote taken from: Dulles, Avery. *The Craft of Theology: From Symbol to System*. Crossroad Publishing, 1995, 160.

regarding the Magi (a conclusion that most serious exegetes and theologians agree on – that the Magi were Astrologers), "This matters because history matters, and history matters because truth matters."[15]

Indeed, the truth does matter. And I believe that modern Christianity's hysteria regarding any spiritual practice that is not rooted in the Judeo-Christian culture is intrinsically counterproductive to the illumination of truth.

In *Nostra Aetate: Declaration on the Relationship of the Church to Non-Christian Religions* (the magisterially binding conciliar declaration– meaning that Catholic Christians are expected to give 'religious assent' to its teachings), the Second Vatican Council states,

> "Humanity forms but one community. This is so because all stem from one stock which God created to people the entire earth (see Acts 17:26), and also because all share a common destiny, namely God. His providence, evident goodness, and saving designs extend to all humankind (see Wis 8:1, Acts 14:17; Rom 2:6-7; 1 Tim 2:4) …
>
> People look to their different religions for an answer to the unsolved riddles of human existence. The problems that weigh heavily on people's hearts are the same today as in past ages. What is humanity? What is the meaning and purpose of life? What is upright behavior, and what is sinful? Where does suffering originate, and what does it serve? How can genuine happiness be found?...

---

15. Longenecker, Dwight. *Mystery of the Magi: The Quest to Identify the Three Wise Men*. First Edition. Washington, D.C: Regnery History, 2017, 159.

Throughout history, to the present day, there is found among different peoples a certain awareness of a hidden power, which lies behind the course of nature and the events of human life. At times, there is present even a recognition of a supreme being, or still more of a Father. The religions which are found in more advanced civilizations endeavor by way of well-defined concepts and exact language to answer these questions. Thus, in Hinduism people explore the divine mystery and express it both in the limitless riches of myth and the accurately defined insights of philosophy. They seek release from the trials of the present life by ascetical practices, profound meditation and recourse to God in confidence and love. Buddhism in its various forms testifies to the essential inadequacy of this changing world… So, too, other religions which are found throughout the world attempt in different ways to overcome the restlessness of people's hearts…

The Catholic Church rejects nothing of what is true and holy in these religions. It has high regard for the manner of life and conduct, the precepts and doctrines which, although differing in many ways from its own teaching, nevertheless often reflect a ray of that truth which enlightens all men and women. Yet it proclaims and is in duty bound to proclaim without fail, **Christ who is the way, the truth and the life** (Jn 1:6). In him, in whom God reconciled all things to himself (see 2 Cor 5:18-19), people find the fullness of their religious life.

FRAMING THE SEARCH FOR TRUTH

The Church, therefore, urges its sons and daughters to enter with prudence and charity into discussion and collaboration with members of other religions. Let Christians, while witnessing to their own faith and way of life, **acknowledge, preserve, and encourage the spiritual and moral truths found among non-Christians,** together with their social life and culture."[16]

(emphasis mine)

Before we begin, there are two more truths that must 'frame' this conversation.

1. This work is in no way meant to 'stick it' to the Christian Church, its leaders, and its followers. I am a Christ-follower first and foremost. I am grateful to share that the Catholic Church has no official or infallible magisterial teachings condemning Astrology. I pray that everyone reading this finds themselves welcomed into the arms of the bride of Christ (his Church) and experiences the most rewarding relationship of all, that of personally knowing and loving our Lord Jesus Christ. I also pray that this book helps comfort and guide those who may have left the Church, and that they feel comfortable to return.

2. While I am welcoming of alternative cultural traditions and practices that have been found to be true, good, and are helpful and useful for this

---

16. Pope Paul VI. "Nostra Aetate: DECLARATION ON THE RELATION OF THE CHURCH TO NON-CHRISTIAN RELIGIONS," October 28, 1965, 1-2.

life on Earth– there is much among the 'New Age' spirituality that is objectively harmful and should be avoided at all costs. Ouija boards, consulting mediums and psychics, and attempting to know and control the future all fall under this category. Nearly all religious traditions agree that attempting to know and control the future, communicate with the dead, and/or any spiritual, physical or sexual practice that includes harm to a person or creature (or seeks to 'use' another's energy in some way) are practices distinctly dangerous to the human soul. Finally, any community that claims to have "secret knowledge" that one may learn only after mastering certain levels or going through various initiations is not operating in the light of truth. I am not condoning <u>any</u> such practices or belief systems.

The intention of this work is to remind the Christian Church that it is in fact the *"pillar and foundation of truth"*[17], while simultaneously reminding her of the deep, abiding love we ought to have for one another. We have nothing to be afraid of in any faith tradition—especially not the numerous cosmological, spiritual and scientific truths which God has given to the various peoples of the world in order to make their journey on Earth easier. I pray that the Christian Church recognizes what it truly means to be 'universal' and welcomes *"what is true and holy"* in other belief systems and cultures without the fear-mongering we find far too often at the mere mention of an unfamiliar practice.

---

17. *NABRE - New American Bible Revised Edition*, 1 Timothy 3:15.

Finally, I pray that the Church and the faithful on social media step away from their fascination with the demonic, and shift toward an intimate relationship with and an abiding love for God, and one another.

2

AN EXEGESIS OF MATTHEW 2:1-12 AND ITS HISTORICAL CONTEXT

Growing up in a hispanic household, we dutifully celebrated "El Dia De Los Reyes", also known as Three Kings Day. My siblings and I would run around the yard filling shoeboxes with grass for the camels- setting them just outside the front door before bed. We excitedly waited for the gifts the Magi would bring to us on our special "second Christmas", as they journeyed past our house on their way to visit the Christ child.

While these details made for a very fun childhood tradition, much has been elaborated on from the original text. It seems as though Christians historically attempted to answer the numerous questions created by the story through folklore. Three kings? It doesn't tell us how many Magi there were, nor that they were kings—only that there were three gifts. There is no mention of camels, or any animals for that matter. From Orient (or one Asian, one Caucasian, and one African)? Matthew only says "from the East".

While pop culture is replete with illustrations of the story of the Magi, it is best to allow history to fill in the blanks. In this chapter we are going to look very closely at the story of the Magi, and see for ourselves the clues Matthew gives us about who they were, and what lessons Christians should glean from the story.

A CLOSE ANALYSIS OF MATTHEW 2:1-12

"We saw his star at its rising and have come to do him homage."[1] These fourteen simple words, spoken by men only described as 'magi from the east', have created numerous questions and inspired an enormous amount of investigation for centuries. Almost since the beginning of Christendom, theologians, historians, and astronomers have debated the content of the star, whether or not the story is fact or fiction, and the identity of the magi. Even St. John Chrysostom, in his *Homily on the Magi* (a sermon given in the late 4th century) acknowledged the overwhelming nature of the questions created by this story, "But lest, stringing questions upon questions, we should be wilder you, come let us now enter upon the solution of the matters inquired of".[2]

Below is the story of the Magi as told in the gospel of Matthew. Let's go over it together, and then I will share reflections line by line. I have bolded certain phrases which will be important to come back to. Emphasis mine.

---

1. Matthew 2:1-12, *NABRE - New American Bible Revised Edition*. Wichita: Catholic Bible Publishers, 2010.
2. Chrysostom, John. "Homilies on the Gospel of Matthew - Dual Parallel English and Original Text." (vi). https://catholiclibrary.org/library/view?docId=Synchronized-EN/Chrysostom.Matthew.en.html;chunk.id=00000013.

(1) When Jesus was born in Bethlehem of Judea, **in the days of King Herod**, behold, **magi from the east** arrived in Jerusalem, (2) saying, "Where is the newborn king of the Jews? We saw **his star at its rising** and have come to do him homage." (3) When King Herod heard this, he was greatly troubled, **and all Jerusalem with him.** (4) Assembling all the **chief priests and the scribes** of the people, he inquired of them where the Messiah was to be born. (5) They said to him, "**In Bethlehem of Judea**, for thus it has been written through the prophet: (6) 'And you, Bethlehem, land of Judah, are by no means least among the rulers of Judah; since from you shall come a ruler, who is to shepherd my people Israel.'" (7) Then Herod called the magi secretly and **ascertained from them the time of the star's appearance.** (8) **He sent them to Bethlehem** and said, "Go and search diligently for the child. When you have found him, bring me word, that I too may go and do him homage." (9) After their audience with the king they set out. And behold, **the star that they had seen at its rising preceded them, until it came and stopped over the place where the child was.** (10) They were overjoyed at seeing the star, (11) and on entering the house they saw the child with Mary his mother. **They prostrated themselves and did him homage**. Then they opened their treasures and offered him gifts of gold, frankincense, and myrrh. (12) And having been warned in a dream not to return to Herod, they

departed for their country by another way.

The story continues in describing the slaughter of the innocents, which is not recorded elsewhere.

Let's begin our exegesis by reviewing what the Bible story actually says.

1. When Jesus was born in Bethlehem of Judea, **in the days of King Herod**, behold, **magi from the east** arrived in Jerusalem,

This first line gives us the specific place that Jesus was born in (differentiating Bethlehem of Judea from Bethlehem of Galilee) when he was born (in the days of King Herod, between 37 BCE and 4 BCE), and who arrived in Jerusalem (Magi- plural of magus, meaning magician or Zoroastrian Priest) from the East (we don't know where, specifically).

(2) saying, "Where is the newborn king of the Jews? We saw **his star at its rising** and have come to do him homage."

Upon arrival, they inquired specifically about the "newborn king of the Jews". So, they knew three very important facts. One, there was a new baby recently born. Two, that baby was a king. Three, that baby was a Jew. They had seen its "star at its rising" (not to be confused with, "we followed the star to Jerusalem"). Without further context, we can only gather that they discerned this information from the 'star' itself, and being that the baby was Jewish they assumed they needed to go to the center of Judaism, Jerusalem. Finally, they "have come to do him homage"—for reasons unknown to us, they have left their homeland to come and to pay their respects to the baby Jewish King.

> (3) When King Herod heard this, he was greatly troubled, **and all Jerusalem with him.**

King Herod is renowned for being suspicious, and like many rulers of his day he was especially manic regarding the usurpation of his throne (he even killed his own sons and wife in his paranoia).[3] So he was troubled for obvious reasons, but Jerusalem was troubled too. This means that the Jewish people, priests and scribes, with all their wisdom and knowledge, did not know that the birth of their Savior had occurred. Interesting.

> (4) Assembling all the **chief priests and the scribes** of the people, he inquired of them where the Messiah was to be born.

Herod was raised a Jew, and knew where to go for information regarding a Jewish prophecy. The Chief Priests and Scribes were known for their extensive training and knowledge of scripture.

> (5) They said to him, "**In Bethlehem of Judea**, for thus it has been written through the prophet: (6) 'And you, Bethlehem, land of Judah, are by no means least among the rulers of Judah; since from you shall come a ruler, who is to shepherd my people Israel.'"

---

3. Burrell, Barbara. 2014. "The Legacies of Herod the Great." *Near Eastern Archaeology* 77 (2): 68–74.

https://doi.org/10.5615/neareastarch.77.2.0068.

<u>Twice</u> Matthew mentions Bethlehem of Judea. He seems to really want his mostly Jewish audience to recognize that this was the fulfillment of the prophecy. Bethlehem of Judea is only five miles southeast of Jerusalem, so the Magi's methods got them <u>very</u> close.[4]

> (7) Then Herod called the magi secretly and **ascertained from them the time of the star's appearance.**

The <u>time</u> of the star's appearance ('rising', as previously noted) was such critical information that it needed to be ascertained *in secret*.

> (8) **He sent them to Bethlehem** and said, "Go and search diligently for the child. When you have found him, bring me word, that I too may go and do him homage."

It is strange that Herod would send the Magi alone to a small town only five miles from Jerusalem. One would think that for such a short trip, Herod would send the Magi with royal accompaniment, or at the very least have spies follow them if he wanted to be less obvious. While still deceitful, this move is out of character for the paranoid Herod.

> (9) After their audience with the king they set out.[5]

---

4. This immediately makes me question the idea of a miraculous star—because why would it take them 5 miles away from their destination?

5. Now, this is speculation- but it appears they set out right after the audience with the king. Without any further context, one could assume that these conversations happened over the course of one day, and the

> And behold, **the star that they had seen at its rising preceded them, until it came and stopped over the place where the child was.**

Whether they left right after the audience with the king, or just 'some time' after (for example, after staying overnight or a meal) is not specified. But the star preceded them in their journey southeast and appeared to stop over the place where the child was.[6]

> (10) They were overjoyed at seeing the star, (11) and on entering the house they saw the child with Mary his mother. **They prostrated themselves and did him homage**. Then they opened their treasures and offered him gifts of gold, frankincense, and myrrh.

They were very happy to have further guidance, and entered a house. This is not the stable/cave in which Mary gave birth, meaning that the Holy Family had found shelter by this time. Therefore, this was likely days, weeks or months (not hours) after the birth of Jesus. Upon entering the house they prostrated (meaning they lied flat on the ground with their face down in a position of worship) and did him homage (a dedication of respect or honor). Then, they gave him valuable gifts.

---

would arrive before nightfall (walking or riding by camel for 5 miles takes about 1-2 hours, depending on terrain). This would support theories we will discuss later regarding the exact astrological phenomenon that scholars believe led the Magi to the Christ-child. However, it doesn't have to. Speculation is not fact, and I will take care in this exegesis not to impose our modern lens into the story

6. This is the first indication of a potentially miraculous event.

These were men who evidently knew the sacred when they saw it.

> (12) And having been warned in a dream not to return to Herod, they departed for their country by another way.

Evidently, they stayed and slept there or somewhere in Bethlehem—because the warning came to them in a dream.[7] Based on this warning, they chose to take another route home, so that Herod would not track them down.

QUESTIONS THE STORY RAISES

Again, we can see after reading the actual text that many details have been 'read into' the story by Church culture and myth. Often we see the Magi portrayed as three men, who all came from various parts of the world on camels, and in the stable just after the time of Jesus' birth. The star is depicted as a magical star that led the Magi to and fro, and no one seems to question the fact that Bethlehem and Jerusalem are only five miles apart. When one approaches the story with a scholar's eye, there are even more inconsistencies. Why do so few other historical documents affirm the story of the Magi or the slaughter of the innocents? Why was the author so vague regarding the origins of the Magi and their intent for visiting the Christ child, contrary to how Luke shares the story of the shepherd in his infancy narrative? Finally, we get to the

---

7. The idea that they stayed the night in Bethlehem rather than traveling the five miles back to Jerusalem supports my theory regarding the end-of-day trek the Magi may have made from Jerusalem to Bethlehem.

ultimate question: Is the story of the Magi even real, or is it simply a legend?

ARE THE MAGI HISTORICAL OR LITERARY FIGURES? A REVIEW OF THE LITERATURE

Most of us assume that the story of the Magi is historical. However, there is not actually widespread scholarly consensus to this end. In the words of Bible Scholar and Jesuit Priest Daniel Harrington, "the question of the historical character of the narratives in Matthew 2 is a complicated issue."[8] Many theologians attest that, although the story of the Magi is not supported by other historical sources, the fact that the writer of Matthew noted the place (Bethlehem of Judea, rather than Bethlehem of Galilee[9]) and time ("in the days of King Herod"[10]) of the events using actual historical figures denotes a historical event rather than an allegorical one.[11] After all, fairy tales tend to begin with, "once upon a time"—not, "in this exact place at this exact time". Raymond Brown makes room for both arguments, concisely stating that "the simplest explanation" of the story of the Magi "is that it is factual history passed down in family circles", while also acknowledging that "those who wish to maintain the historicity of the Matthean magi story are faced with nigh insuperable obstacles."[12]

---

8. Harrington, Daniel J., *Sacra Pagina: The Gospel of Matthew*. Collegeville, Minn: Liturgical Press, 2007, p. 46.
9. Harrington, p. 41.
10. Matthew 2:1, *NABRE*.
11. See Thomas Aquinas, *Catena Aurea*, p. 62 and Benedict XVI, *The Infancy Narratives*, p. 89.
12. Brown, Raymond E. *The Birth of the Messiah*. Updated edition. New York: Anchor Bible, 1993, p. 188.

These obstacles are, in fact, nigh insuperable. Brown started with the star, as an intrinsic unlikelihood. "A star that rose in the East, appeared over Jerusalem, turned South to Bethlehem, and then came to rest over a house would have constituted a celestial phenomenon unparalleled in astronomical history; yet it received no notice in the records of the times"[13] and notes that the story does not state that only the Magi saw the star. He also mentions that Herod did not send anyone to follow the Magi on their 5-mile journey, as neurotic as he was, and points out the probable impression the "exotic magi from the East with royal gifts" would have made on a tiny village... and yet rather than easily discovering which house the child had resided in from locals or spies, Herod rather chose to slaughter all of the male children under the age of two in an event which itself was not recorded in the accounts of contemporary historians, even those who specifically covered Herod's reign. Finally, the stories conflict with other accounts in the New Testament, namely Luke's version of the infancy narrative.[14] Roy Kotanasky agrees, stating, "One of the greatest difficulties ... is the extent to which one can accept the truthfulness of this famous Christmas story... historians see little that is not legendary in this account."[15]

However, Harrington is not so quick to dismiss the Magi. "For their historicity one can point to many features that are compatible with what is known from other sources: the character of Herod the Great, Jewish interest in astrology,

---

13. Brown, p. 188.
14. Brown, p. 189.
15. Kotansky, Roy. "The Star of the Magi: Lore and Science in Ancient Zoroastrianism, the Greek Magical Papyri, and St Matthew's Gospel." *Annali Di Storia Dell'Esegesi* 24, no. 2 (July 2007), p. 379.

Egypt as a place of refuge for Jews, etc." He concludes by acknowledging, "The historicity of these episodes remains an open question that probably can never be definitely decided. The more important issue is determining what these stories meant to Matthew and his community."[16] More recently, there are documents being discovered that may confirm Jesus' childhood in Egypt—which would give more credence to the story. Contrary to what Harrington states above, I actually do believe that we may one day have a definitive answer. But today is not that day. What we do know, though, is that Matthew chose to use valuable papyrus to share the story—which means that even if the story isn't perfectly historical, it is important.

So why would the author of Matthew choose to include such a story, *especially* if it isn't factual? What did it mean to Matthew and his community? We will now attempt to answer these questions.

WHO WROTE THE BOOK OF MATTHEW?

Historically, it has been taken for granted that the Apostle Matthew wrote the Gospel that bears his name. However, over the last century as the Church adopted the historical-critical method of exegesis, most scholars came to believe that the Gospel of Matthew was written between AD 80 and 90 by an anonymous author. Exegete Raymond E. Brown says as much— "Most scholars today maintain that the Gospel was written in Syria by an unknown Greek-speaking Jewish Christian, living in the 80s in a mixed community with converts of both Jewish and Gentile

---

16. Harrington, p. 47.

descent."[17] But things have once again changed. New discoveries show that it could have been composed as early as the 40s or 50s AD—and this has brought many scholars back around to the notion that the author was in fact the apostle Matthew.[18] [19] Personally, I agree with this latter argument. The position is strengthened by what we know about the author based on the clues given in the Gospel: "He shows a special interest in the Hebrew Scriptures as a witness to the person and activity of Jesus... he also seems familiar with Jewish traditions of interpretation"[20] Harrington notes, citing Matthew 5:34-35, 23:16-22, and 27:51-53 as examples. Indeed, we know that Matthew the Tax Collector[21] was raised a Jew, and would have been familiar with these histories.

POSSIBLE MOTIVATIONS FOR MATTHEW TO INCLUDE THE STORY OF THE MAGI

Matthew began his ministry preaching in Judea, before moving East. Scholars also note that Matthew was intentional about making parallels between Jesus Christ and the Messianic prophecies in the Old Testament. Jews who had converted to Christianity would have had a particular interest in making parallels between Jesus and the Old Testament, in order to support the claim that Jesus was in fact the Messiah of the Old Testament. It is well known that the author of Hebrews exaggerated Melchizedek's resemblance to Christ as an analogy for the

---

17. Brown, p. 45.
18. Pitre, Brant, and Robert Barron. 2016. *The Case for Jesus: The Biblical and Historical Evidence for Christ*. Image, 12.
19. Harrington, p. 8.
20. Harrington, p. 9.
21. Matthew 9:9-10

priesthood, seemingly for the same purpose.[22] Harrington specifies the similarities that were made between Moses and Jesus, "In both cases a wicked king tried to do away with them as infants, their escape was accompanied by a slaughter of innocent children; and return became possible only after those who sought the child's life had died."[23] These parallels require the story of the Magi—which is only present in Matthew's infancy narrative, not Luke's. This theory implies that the story is an exaggeration to manufacture additional parallels between the Old and New Testament, and make Jesus as the Messiah more believable to the Jews converting in Judea. As you can imagine, acquiescing to this theory puts the validity of Christ as the Messiah in question.

For this very reason, many disagree with this theory—not least because it is speculation. Presbyterian Theologian D. Mark Davis, quotes Bible Scholars William Albright and C.S. Mann, "'What seems to us to be wholly inadmissible is the suggestion that Matthew was so anxious to represent Jesus as the new Moses . . . that the evangelist has constructed an allegory which includes Gentiles (the magi)' (Albright and Mann, Matthew, 15)".[24] I agree with this assertion. An outright fabrication of the Magi simply to portray Jesus as a 'Moses-figure' seems far-fetched and unnecessary.[25]

Another plausible reason to include a non-historical narrative would be to present the Magi as a model for

---

22. Hebrews 7, NABRE.
23. Harrington, p. 49.
24. Davis, D Mark. "Matthew 2:1-12." *Interpretation* 57, no. 4 (October 2003), p. 421.
25. With all of this being said, my personal opinion is that the story is factual and did happen as told.

Gentiles who were converting to the faith. Matthew is known as 'Matthew the Evangelist' (alongside the other three gospel writers, Mark, Luke, and John). In the words of New Testament Scholar and Theologian Eugene Boring: "'The magi are Gentiles in the extreme, characters who could not be more remote from the Jewish citizens of Jerusalem in heritage and worldview' (E. Boring, Matthew, NIB, vol. VIII [Nashville: Abingdon, 1995] 145)."[26] Perhaps Matthew hoped that including Gentiles in the infancy narrative would support those considering converting to the faith. This would not be completely off base, as Matthew distinctly focused heavily on evangelism in his writings. Harrington reminds us, "Matthew's Gospel ends with the risen Lord's command to 'make disciples of all the nations' (28:19)" and adds another literary perspective— "Matthew sets up a deliberate contrast between the Gentile Magi who sincerely wish to pay homage to the 'king of the jews' and Herod who claims to be 'king of the jews'".[27] Indeed, the Magi's shameless seeking of the Christ-child, followed by prostrating themselves and doing him homage, and finally—the laying down of gifts before him and his mother represent a model of worship which has reverberated profoundly across time. The Magi are still held up as a model for Christians today, two thousand years later. It is not far-fetched to think they were held up as an example for conversion then, too.

Unfortunately, 'motivation' cannot be proven or disproven definitively. We can only conclude that it appears Matthew used this story for multiple purposes. The first purpose seems to be to note the time and place of Jesus' birth, since he was so intentional about including these facts. The

---
26. Davis, p. 421.
27. Harrington, p. 49.

second seems to be to offer a sort of apologetical argument for the newly converted Jewish-Christian population, and to ensure that various aspects of the prophecies are fulfilled.[28] Finally, there is a sort of modeling for Gentile believers, and for evangelization. Raymond Brown notes that Matthew is "hinting that Jesus was destined for the Gentiles as well as the Jews..."[29]. This is an important distinction to make, considering that it was mostly Gentiles who were converting at that moment in time, likely not least due to the fact that "in Matthew's time the Pharisee authorities in the Synagogue were hostile to the claims made for Jesus..."[30]. This means that to be an apostle of Jesus as one born a Jew, a part of your contribution to the church was "one of going and making disciples of the Gentiles"[31]—that is, one of educating the Gentiles of the Jewish background of the Christian faith. Along that vein, perhaps the author of Matthew included the story in the infancy narratives for the purpose of emphasizing the following message: that the salvific gift of Christ was one meant for the entire world, not just the 'chosen' people.[32]

The message is clear—Gentiles were to be welcomed alongside Jewish converts. As you can see, the actual biblical story is very different from the pop culture representation of the Magi.[33] Unfortunately, we may never

---

28. *"May the kings of Tarshish and of distant shores bring tribute to him. May the kings of Sheba and Seba present him gifts. May all kings bow down to him..."* — Psalm 72:10–11; and *"A multitude of camels shall cover you... They shall bring gold and frankincense, and shall proclaim the praise of the Lord."*— Isaiah 60:6
29. Brown, p. 181.
30. Brown, p. 182.
31. Brown, p. 182.
32. We will explore the implications of this for ecumenism and evangelization later in the paper.
33. Don't worry, I'm not removing the Magi from my nativity scene, either.

know if the story of the Magi is fact or fiction, or why it was included in the Gospel. What we do know is that it is a story that was selected by Matthew as imperative to the retelling of the birth of Jesus Christ—which makes the study of the Magi story an honorable task for the Christian. If nothing else, as the first known Gentiles to convert to Christianity in history— the Magi— can give us invaluable insights into the intended journey of the Christian.

3

WHO WERE THE MAGI, AND WHAT WAS THE STAR?

Although my husband has always been supportive of my research, it would be wrong to assume that he has never given me pushback, in particular of my study of astrology.

"If astrology is true, that would mean a lot of people are wrong" he would challenge me, like every good spouse does—"I know you are studying this stuff… but why has God given *you* this message to share?"

His questions were valid.

The truth is, I am the last person to question the Church. Before I went to school for Theology, I was a suburban stay at home Mom who had no background in any of this. So often throughout this journey, I have felt like Moses— "Who am I that I should go to Pharaoh and lead the Israelites out of Egypt?"[1]

Yet, my response to this line of questioning is simple. At the end of the day, I just can't ignore God. For years, I

---

1. Exodus 3:11

have felt an unmistakable call to continue my research, to continue studying astrology, and to move forward in discerning the truth. Even though I sometimes wish I could just be a normal wife and mom (and not the person who has to 'warn' every new Pastor about my studies and work online)—I also know what it feels like to witness one's mission so clearly, and to know that it would be a profound self-betrayal to stay silent. Maybe you know what this feels like, too.

I imagine this is how it felt for the Magi. Because honestly —why would they leave their home to go to a foreign land to visit a newborn King? Some speculate that they were sent as ambassadors for another regent. Regardless of who they were, *someone* became <u>so</u> convicted by what they saw, that they chose to undertake a potentially costly and dangerous journey out of their homeland to visit the Christ-child.

WHO WERE THE MAGI?

The term Magi is plural of the word "Magus", and refers to a group who were trained as priests or magicians within the pagan religions of the Ancient Middle East, specifically Zoroastrianism.

Unfortunately, the question "who *specifically* were the Magi?" has proved yet another difficult question to answer. Davis acknowledges, "Partly because of the 'cameo' nature of the magi's appearance, there is considerable confusion regarding who they are."[2] Pope Benedict XVI (writing as Joseph Ratzinger), states that the Magi were members of

---

2. Davis, 420.

the Persian priestly caste,[3] but notes that perhaps the uncertainty of the Magi's identity in the story is intentional. "The ambivalence of the concept of the Magi that we find here illustrates the ambivalence of religion in general."[4] What the word only tells us for sure, is that there were more than one.

REVIEW OF THE LITERATURE

While the precise historical identification of the Magi is outside of the possibility of this work, we can make a good guess via a review of both ancient and modern theological opinion regarding what type of people they were. Truthfully, there is very little argument on this subject. The evidence is overwhelming. Jesuit Priest and former Georgetown University Professor David J. Collins, SJ even hints at this fact when discussing 13th Century Theologian and Doctor of the Church St. Albert the Great, "He started with the theological opinion held since Christian antiquity that the magi were not sorcerers but legitimate astrologers."[5] Theophylact, 11th Century Byzantine Archbishop and Biblical Scholar says the following, "the Magi were astrologers, and so the Lord used what was familiar to them to draw them to himself.. "[6] [7] In modern

---

3. Pope Benedict XVI. *Jesus of Nazareth: The Infancy Narratives*. Image, 2012, 92.
4. Benedict XVI, 93.
5. Collins, David J. 2024. *Disenchanting Albert the Great: The Life and Afterlife of a Medieval Magician*. Penn State University Press, 40.
6. Allison, Jr., Dale C. 2012. *Studies in Matthew: Interpretation Past and Present*. Reprint edition. Baker Academic, 31.
7. In this case he is referencing a miraculous star phenomenon, not an astrological phenomenon, but we will debunk this claim later in the chapter. The important thing is the acknowledgement that the Magi were Astrologers.

times, Pope Francis stated publicly that the Magi were astrologers in a homily on the Epiphany, and continued to speak exceptionally highly of their journey as an example for all Christians.[8] In *'Sacra Pagina'*, his exegesis on the book of Matthew, New Testament Scholar Daniel J. Harrington, SJ writes, "Here they appear as astrologers/astronomers who looked to the movement of the stars as a guide to major events."[9] Finally, Raymond Brown agrees, "Matthew's description of the magi as interpreting the rise of a star tips the scales in favor of his considering them to be astrologers."[10]

Overwhelmingly, the conclusion of modern scripture scholars and theologians alike is that the Magi were either real or fictitious astrologers. This is found to be true in less academic (but still rigorous) inquiries as well. Dwight Longenecker states the following in his book *Mystery of the Magi*, "Although they were astrologers, the Magi really did look to the heavens for guidance... The Magi's whole world view and cosmology were predicated upon a belief that the 'heavens declare the glory of God and the firmament shows his handiwork' (Psalm 19). They believed the whole of creation was an interlocking system and by studying one part you could discern the hand of God in another."[11]

Not only were the Magi (according to most) definitively astrologers, but they were *good*. This point matters, because many will attempt to portray the Magi as sinners and

---

8. Pope Francis. "Holy Mass on the Solemnity of the Epiphany of the Lord," January 6, 2022.
9. Harrington, 42.
10. Brown, 167.
11. Longenecker, Dwight. 2017. *Mystery of the Magi: The Quest to Identify the Three Wise Men*. First Edition. Regnery History. 163-164.

diviners who abandoned their practices after encountering Christ. This assertion has no basis in scripture and is pure speculation. Fr. Raymond Brown denounces the apologists who give opinions on the magi with the intent of denouncing their astrology and the occult aspects of their practice, "such references reflect a Christian use of Matthew in an apologetic against magic rather than a true exegesis of Matthew. There is not the slightest hint of conversion or of false practice in Matthew's description of the magi; they are wholly admirable. They represent the best of pagan lore and religious perceptivity which has come to seek Jesus through revelation in nature."[12] Joseph Ratzinger observes, "The men of whom Matthew speaks were not just astronomers. They were 'wise'. They represent the inner dynamic of religion towards self-transcendence, which involved a search for truth, a search for the true God and hence "philosophy" in the original sense of the word."[13] Harrington also notes that the Magi were portrayed positively in Matthew, as opposed to the negative portrayal of Egyptian magicians.[14]

All in all, they are portrayed as good, and wise Astrologers. Despite the many questions left unanswered by both scriptural exegesis and historical study alike, this seems to be the one opinion on which experts can agree.

With that in mind, we will proceed to the question of the nature of the star.

---

12. Brown, p. 167-168.
13. Benedict XVI, 95.
14. Harrington, p. 48.

WHAT WAS THE STAR?

Truthfully, if the story is a fictional tale, then the star can be whatever Matthew wanted it to be. However, there is such a thing as 'intrinsic likelihood'. The nature of the star depends highly on the sort of men the magi were. Considering that the Magi were astrologers, it is *intrinsically likely* that the 'star' is an astrological phenomenon. However, for the sake of hermeneutical accuracy, we will give each position its due.

WAS THE STAR A MIRACULOUS EVENT?

In response to this question, there is a host of Patristic writings. It seems the Early Church was quite taken by the star and required much commentary. In *Ancient Christian Commentary on Matthew*, Editors Simonetti et al. show that most of the early Church Fathers believed that the star mentioned in the Gospel reading was a true, miraculous star created specifically for the purpose of announcing Christ. By subscribing to this literal line of thinking, it appears they sought to distance the Magi from their astrology, which many early Church Fathers were against.[15] However, even astrologically inclined theologians took this position. Famed Theologian, Philosopher, Saint and Doctor of the Church Thomas Aquinas agreed, and in his 'Commentary on Saint Matthew's Gospel' argued that it was a true star, not an astronomical or archeological phenomenon.[16] Even modern Theologian Dale C. Allison

---

15. Simonetti, Manlio, Thomas C. Oden, Christine Caine, and Oden, eds. *Ancient Christian Commentary on Scripture; Matthew 1-13: Volume 1A*. First Edition. Downers Grove, Illinois: IVP Academic, 2001, pgs. 20-30.
16. Larcher, OP, R.F. "Thomas Aquinas Commentary on Saint Matthew's Gospel." https://isidore.co/aquinas/SSMatthew.htm#2 (2-2).

Jr. supports the idea of a miraculous phenomenon, stating in his book, *Studies in Matthew*, "Matthew 2 speaks of a light appearing, disappearing, and reappearing, of it going before the magi, and of it eventually stopping over the place where Jesus is."[17] However his opinion differs slightly from Early Church Fathers in that he makes the case for the Star of Bethlehem being an angel, (rather than a star) despite one not being mentioned in the story.[18]

Allison concludes his case with the following admonition: that most modern exegetes "have shied away from a literal reading of Matthew's text and instead substituted modern science." He offers a possible explanation for the discrepancy, "The resolution to the question lies, I submit, in an all-important distinction between ancient and modern conceptions of the heavenly bodies. Quite simply, Matthew's idea of a star was not our idea of a star... We should not read ourselves into the past."[19]

While it is true that the phenomenon could not have been an *actual* star (which would have consumed the earth before it got too close) by insisting on a miraculous phenomenon in a story where something supernatural is not explicitly stated, one would be doing exactly what Allison warns not to do. Additionally, Herod et al were surprised when the Magi turned up in Jerusalem discussing this star... however if there would have been this bright beautiful star/angel in the sky... wouldn't everyone have seen it? Or could only the Wise Men see it? Why would a miraculous star have led the Wise Men off course, to Jerusalem rather

---

17. Allison, Jr., Dale C. *Studies in Matthew: Interpretation Past and Present*. Reprint edition. Baker Academic, 2012, (p. 21).
18. Allison, pgs. 26- 29.
19. Allison, Jr., Dale C. *Studies in Matthew: Interpretation Past and Present*. Reprint edition. Baker Academic, 2012, (p. 21).

than to Bethlehem, (only five miles away) a pit stop which allegedly resulted in the murder of many infants?

As you can see, the questions keep stacking up. It seems the idea of a miraculous phenomenon leads to much speculation, which we try to avoid when we are trying to discover the truth. I am supported by Brown, who acknowledges how commonplace it was for there to be 'signs in the sky', "the thesis that at least the births and deaths of great men were marked by heavenly signs was widely accepted."[20] Basically, we don't need to insist on miracles to make the story make sense.[21]

SUPERNOVA OR COMET?

Thoughts of a supernova or similar astronomical phenomenon have been explored with some support, most notably by those who place Jesus' birthdate earlier than most theologians and historians, in 12 BCE.[22] [23] Were Jesus to have been born in this year, Halley's comet would have been the significant astronomical event that Matthew was most likely referring to. There are no supernovas recorded during the years in which we believe Christ was born.[24]

Where the comet/alternative astronomical event theory falls short is in the *interpretation* of such a phenomena. How would Halley's comet communicate to the Magi that they needed to go visit the newborn king of the Jews? Comets

---

20. Brown, p. 170.
21. The idea of a "star that went before them and stopped at the place where the child was" has an astronomical explanation, which I will address shortly.
22. Kotansky, p. 384.
23. Most place Christ's birth between 7 and 4 BCE.
24. Brown, p. 171.

actually tend to mark doom and gloom, not good tidings of great joy. Brown states, "a comet was usually thought to herald a catastrophe, so it would be unusual to interpret its appearance as heralding the birth of a salvific figure" and continues to explain that 12 BCE is is very long before the date of 7 or 6 BCE typically assigned for Jesus' birth.[25] It seems we can take both comets and supernovas off the table.

ASTROLOGICAL EVENT?

For these reasons, most who tackle this question come to the conclusion that because *observation* of the phenomena <u>and</u> *interpretation* is necessary, an astrological event is the most likely theory. Ratzinger, for his part, prefers the hypothesis of an astrological conjunction to both place Jesus' birth and provide reasoning for the Magi's journey, quoting astronomy as the support for this position:[26] "Astronomer Ferrari d'Occhieppo has dismissed the theory of a supernova. For him a sufficient explanation of the star of Bethlehem is provided by the conjunction of Jupiter and Saturn in the constellation Pisces…"[27] Brown explores the comet, supernova, and astrological conjunction theories, and recognizes the "rare triple conjunction" of Jupiter and Saturn (a conjunction which some say represents the Jewish religion)[28] in the sign of Pisces (the sign of God, represented symbolically as the fishes). He acknowledges what other theologians, historians and exegetes say about this historical conjunction, and even goes so far as to share

---

25. Brown, 172.
26. Benedict XVI, p. 94.
27. Benedict XVI, p. 99
28. Campion, Nicholas. 2009. *A History of Western Astrology Volume II: The Medieval and Modern Worlds*. Continuum. 59.

some later Jewish support for the messianic interpretation of this very conjunction:

> "Abraham Bar Hiyya (ca. AD 1100) thought that the phenomenon occurred every 2,859 years (actually it occurs every 257 years). He expected that the Messiah would appear before the next conjunction which was to occur in AD 1464. The next conjunction occurred during the lifetime of Isaac Abravanel (1437-1508) who was deeply interested in the coming of the Messiah... It is interesting that Abravanel did not know that the phenomenon to which he gave such attention had occurred just before Jesus' birth."[29]

While it may seem as though a conjunction that happens every 257 years is too common to announce the birth of the long-awaited Messiah, a three-time conjunction followed by the addition of Mars to the party just two months later (perhaps a sort of "time to get moving!" call to the Magi) is more rare.

Longenecker lays out the clearest case, also thoroughly exploring each option (comet, supernova, miraculous event, or astrological phenomenon) and concluding with the following, "With three of the four solutions seeming improbable, we are left with the astrological explanation. According to this theory, the "star" was not a spectacular astronomical display but an alignment of the planets that astrologers interpreted as a sign that a child who would rule over the Jewish people was about to be born."[30]

---

29. Brown, 173.
30. Longenecker, 115.

ASTRONOMICAL SUPPORT

To give the devil his due, Brown—who was particularly devoted to the historical-critical method of exegesis during his time—adds this qualifier, (I have added a few clarifiers in *italics*) "... all of this is very speculative; for we really have no contemporary *(historical)* evidence justifying this reference *(of the star)* to such a conjunction of planets as a 'star' or attaching a particular astrological effect to it, even if there is later Jewish support for that."[31] However, he contradicts himself in his own book. If you flip all the way back to page 611, he (like Ratzinger before him) refers to Austrian Astronomer Ferrari-D'Occhieppo who suggests that the Magi:

> "observed on September 15, 7 B.C. the planetary conjunction of Jupiter and Saturn. On Nov. 12 of that year, as they went from Jerusalem to Bethlehem, Jupiter appeared 50 degrees above the horizon in the direction they were going (and thus apparently going before them)."[32]

D'Occhieppo also attempts some explanations regarding the axis of light at various degrees to make the conjunction appear as though it had stopped over the house of Jesus—but these are a bit too far fetched for me to include. I don't think we need to bend over backwards to make the evidence fit. I also don't necessarily agree with the dates proposed, which insinuate that Jesus was born on September 15th. To me,[33] it appears more likely that the

---

31. Brown, p. 173.
32. Brown, 611-612.
33. Note that this too, is speculation.

Magi observed the three conjunctions throughout the course of the year, realized what they meant, and embarked on their journey in the year 6 BCE. When they turned towards Bethlehem at dusk, the conjunction (which would have been visible in the evening) would have looked like one big star, and would have been a sight to behold, in particular for those in ancient days when they did not suffer from light pollution.[34]

Based on what has been presented here, it seems the logical conclusion is that it is most likely that the star Matthew was referring to is actually the rare three-time astrological conjunction of Jupiter and Saturn in the sign of Pisces—which fits the time, place, the character of the Magi, and the astrological interest of the contemporary culture.

KEY TAKEAWAYS

We have covered a lot in the last two chapters, so let's quickly summarize what we've learned.

1. While we do not know for sure if the story of the Magi is historical or fictional, we do know that Matthew made an intentional decision to include the story in his Gospel.
2. Matthew was a Jewish convert to Christianity with a special interest in evangelism ("Go, therefore, and make disciples of all nations, baptizing them in the name of the Father, and of the Son, and of the Holy Spirit" Matthew 28:19).
3. Most scholars agree that the Magi were

---

34. "The 'Great' Conjunction of Jupiter and Saturn - NASA," December 15, 2020. https://www.nasa.gov/solar-system/the-great-conjunction-of-jupiter-and-saturn/.

astrologers and that the star was *most likely* an astrological phenomenon.
4. Scholars agree the Magi were presented in the gospel as admirable characters.
5. The inclusion of the story of the Magi seems to be for multiple purposes: to mark the birth of Jesus in history, to perhaps draw some parallels between Jesus and Moses, and finally, as an example of how Christ came to save the whole world.

Another Very Important Thing to Acknowledge: the Magi's spirituality got them close, but it only took them so far—they had to ask the Jewish Priests and scribes to get those final five miles to Christ. Astrology (or any other spiritual practice) is not sufficient in and of itself—only God can bring you lasting fulfillment and salvation.

These conclusions lead to many implications, some of which may be difficult for the average Christian to accept. We will spend the following chapters exploring and testing these implications as we continue to wrestle with the ultimate question, is Astrology the 'report that goes forth through all the earth'?

4

ASTROLOGY

PAGAN PRACTICE OR THE 'REPORT THAT GOES FORTH THROUGHOUT ALL THE EARTH?'

"The heavens declare the glory of God; the firmament proclaims the works of his hands. Day unto day pours forth speech; night unto night whispers knowledge. There is no speech, no words; their voice is not heard; a report goes forth through all the earth, their messages, to the ends of the world." - Psalm 19:2-5

I will never forget the moment I realized that Covid-19 was going to change the world as we knew it.

It was March 15, 2020. I was sitting in a restaurant with my dear friend, Jessica. It was a Sunday evening, and as busy moms and wives (who also owned small businesses) we were enjoying a night off and time to catch up. While we were aware of the buzz that had been going around regarding the virus, we were so engulfed in the busy-ness of our lives (and so aware of the death of true journalism) that we did not take the allegations seriously.

We think very similarly (politically and otherwise) and so we both looked with shock at the waiter who informed us that the eat-in aspect of the restaurant would be closing, and that they would only be open for take-out for the foreseeable future. My jaw dropped. "They are shutting down businesses?" I asked in disbelief.

Immediately my mind went to the stories I'd heard from my grandparents, who had escaped communist Cuba in the sixties. They had lived through it all. They had seen Castro's rise, and the exact manipulative tactics he used to turn the people against the rich, law enforcement, and their leaders. My great uncles, extended cousins, and family-members had been jailed and exiled for resisting the communists. After Castro won, the revolutionaries came to their homes to take account of each of their belongings, assess their value and take many things with them as part of a socialist redistribution campaign. My family had watched with their own eyes as their beautiful country fell to the despair it is experiencing now.

Maybe it was because of those very stories I'd heard since childhood— but I immediately saw through the plandemic. The moment I heard the news, my mind went to the fact that it was an election year, there had been no wars, and that we were in a bull market. "They are trying to crash the economy" I realized, as I drove home and saw the lights go off on businesses who did not know when they would re-open, or how they were going to survive. Many of them did not.

I wondered if this would be the beginning of the end for America.

One thing I knew, however, was that the Catholic Church would always stand strong in the face of evil. "God will win" I comforted myself as I parked my car in our apartment complex, "We will be fine." I went to bed that night knowing that no matter what, the Church would not falter.

And then, the unthinkable happened. The Churches closed.

By government order, we stopped having access to the sacraments. Church leaders, and even the Pope himself supported this. I could not believe my eyes.

This was an important moment for me. This was the moment I realized that the Church can be mistaken, too. While the gates of hell will never prevail against the Church[1], its members can unwittingly (or wittingly) go along with the devil's schemes. I was a child when the sexual scandals in the Church were exposed, and my parents had shielded me from much of it. 2020 was the first time that I had seen ignorance in the Church so clearly. 2020 is when I realized, if the Church was wrong about Covid, they could be wrong about Astrology.

I decided I was done keeping myself willfully ignorant while Churches were forced to shut their doors and stop offering soul-saving sacraments.

As a good Catholic, I had previously told my Astrologer that I only wanted to hear about my natal chart, and the charts of family members in our sessions. 'Mundane' Astrology (which is reading the charts of the world (*mundo* = world), and various nations and their leaders) felt a little bit too messy and had too much of a danger of leaning into prediction for me to feel comfortable.

But that was before the world lost its mind. Everything changed when the Pope went along with the circus.

---

1. Matthew 16:18

I went straight to my next astrology session, and deployed my potty mouth. "What the f*** is going on?!"

She sighed.

"Yeah, it's rough," she acknowledged. "Astrologers have been looking at 2020 since the 90s. So much is happening here, but it is good. The truth will be revealed. This is the beginning of the end for those who have been operating in darkness for far too long."[2]

Her words reminded me of a vision that I had heard about Pope Leo XIII (the 13th, not our current Pope, Leo XIV). Apparently while at mass in 1884, he was allowed to witness a conversation between God and Satan, where Satan was requesting 75 to 100 years in which to destroy the Catholic Church. Exact details of the story differ, but some say that God gave the devil the opportunity to select a century to do his worst. he chose the Twentieth Century.[3]

But it is always darkest just before dawn, and the truth will always be revealed. Satan's time has come to an end.

It is God's time now. And sometimes, you have to destroy before you can rebuild. For those who knew how to read

---

2. I want to drive home this point. As you can see by the way my astrologer spoke about the 2020s- the 'forecasts' that astrologers get access to are not specific attempts to view and see the future, it is a very general look into what the energy will feel like based on what the energy has felt like in the past. This is akin to my knowledge that the weather in Utah is the best in May and September, which I know based on my experiences living there. We just get the benefit of thousands of years of 'experience' when it comes to astrology. Saying 'the truth will be revealed' does not mean she knew what the truth was, who was going to reveal it, or even when specifically. She was as shocked by the covid lockdowns as I was.

3. Tremblay, Joe. 2013. "The 100 Year Test." Catholic News Agency. https://www.catholicnewsagency.com/column/52453/the-100-year-test.

the 'report that goes forth through all the earth' (which unfortunately, was very few Christians), it was simply a matter of watching, waiting, and trusting.

"Tell me everything," I said to my Astrologer, "I'm ready to hear it."

IN EVERY TIME AND AT EVERY PLACE, GOD DRAWS CLOSE TO MAN
[4]

The privilege of distancing ourselves from the movement of the celestial bodies is one only known to Modern Man. Anyone who has picked up a Farmer's Almanac knows that an integral part of farming, growing crops, and living a life in line with the cycles of the earth is heavily influenced by the positions and signs of the Moon. For decades, Farmers have looked to the lunar cycles to discover the best time to mow, prune, harvest and beyond. The Moon gave integral information for survival to Native Americans, leading to them naming each Moon according to events that took place or needed to take place around that time.[5] April's full moon was called the 'Pink Moon' because it heralded the appearance of the Moss pink, or wild ground phlox, one of the first spring flowers. June's full moon was called the 'Strawberry Moon' because it appeared when the strawberry harvest took place. September's full moon was called the 'Corn Moon' because this was the time to harvest corn.

---

4. Ratzinger, Joseph Cardinal. 1995. *Catechism of the Catholic Church*. Image, Doubleday, 1.
5. *The Old Farmer's Almanac*. 2024. Vol. 232. Yankee Publishing Incorporated, 259.

Our Western culture is replete with words of astrological origin that we use every day, especially to mark dates. Sunday is obvious. Did you know that Monday is named for the moon? (*lundi*- french, *lunes*- Spanish) Or that Saturday means Saturn's day? While to us in the modern age, Christianity and Astrology seem to be concepts that are completely foreign to one another, this has not been true for the majority of Christianity's existence.

For nearly two millennia, Christianity and Astrology have experienced a sort of tenuous coexistence. While their relationship has certainly had its ups and downs, they have never been far apart. We are now in a moment in history when Christians are rekindling their interest in Astrology, and are once again wondering if it could possibly be a way to communicate with God.

There is much to be said for this line of thinking. From St. Albert the Great and Thomas Aquinas to Hildegard of Bingen, we find evidence of the Christian Church's belief in Astrology from a theological perspective. From Plato[6] to Nicholas Campion, we have the historical and philosophical evidence. There is even burgeoning physical and scientific evidence that the planets could, in fact, influence the lives of those on earth.

> "There is highly statistically significant evidence for a causal relationship between the power spectra of the planetary torque (of Jupiter) on the Sun and the

---

6. Plato, Robin Waterfield, and Andrew Gregory. 2008. *Timaeus and Critias*. Oxford University Press.

observed magnetic activity at the solar surface as derived from cosmogenic radionuclides."[7] [8]

THE PHILOSOPHY FROM WHICH WE APPROACH TRUTH

In order for something to be considered convincingly true, we like to see it be supported in at least two categories of knowledge. The first is from a theological, philosophical, and/or moral perspective; and the second, a historical, mathematical, and/or scientific perspective. Like a system of checks and balances, these categories support one another and maintain honesty in any discipline. This is particularly important in more esoteric disciplines like theology, which is as subject to honest mistakes, ideological narcissism and/or legalism as any other entity run by men. A church may say something is true or not true, but if the historical or scientific evidence says otherwise, we often must conclude that the church is wrong. Over the history of the Christian Church, we have had to acquiesce to such evidence many times- such as in regards to the placement of the Earth in the solar system, the intellect of women, and the age of the Earth- the Church has acknowledged error in light of scientific advancement.

I believe that such may be the case for Astrology.

---

7. Abreu, J. A., J. Beer, A. Ferriz-Mas, K. G. McCracken, and F. Steinhilber. 2012. "Is There a Planetary Influence on Solar Activity?" *Astronomy & Astrophysics* 548 (December): A88, 6. https://doi.org/10.1051/0004-6361/201219997.

8. Basically, this means that it is possible that Jupiter's torque causes sun storms, and we know that storms on the sun affect human behavior here on earth. The science is primitive, but it's burgeoning. However, we are not relying on the physical sciences in this arguement, but rather on history.

Along the same vein, it is worthwhile to note that science has also proved religion. From the Priest-discovered Big Bang Theory, to the Catholic Church's position on contraception (and the outrage of women who have discovered that they've been fed a group one carcinogen for half a century)[9], to the 'Case for Christ'[10], to Quantum Physics, science has also had to acknowledge that what religion and ancient spiritual traditions knew for centuries plays out in the physical realm. Again, it is a system of checks and balances, on both sides of the equation.

The Magi have given us a robust theological case. Here, I will touch on a few theological sources but will focus on history to give evidence and create a case for the thesis that Astrology is a language God uses to communicate with us. But first, lets define some terms.

WHAT DO I MEAN WHEN I REFER TO 'ASTROLOGY'?

Many attempt to disprove Astrology because of a slight secondary rotation which creates the Earth's tilt and causes the sign behind the sun at its rising to change slowly over time (also known as the precession of the equinoxes). This means that the sun is no longer rising in any given sign when we say it is, and this will continue to change more and more over time—making astrology less and less 'astronomically correct' as time goes on. This is why you can find scientists and astronomers online insisting that

---

9. "Oral Contraceptives (Birth Control Pills) and Cancer Risk - NCI." 2018. cgvArticle. March 1. https://www.cancer.gov/about-cancer/causes-prevention/risk/hormones/oral-contraceptives-fact-sheet.
10. Strobel, Lee. 2000. *The Case for Christ: A Journalist's Personal Investigation of the Evidence for Jesus*. Zondervan.

astrology has absolutely no basis in reality, because it is not scientifically accurate. There is merit to this argument if we were talking about the physical sciences only. Again, if we were following the actual movements of the planets, all of the signs would fall on different days than they do currently.

However, this is an incorrect way to approach Astrology. Astrology as the *logos* (word) of the stars is both a calendar and a language. It is not an astronomical (astronomy= astro- *nomy*- the 'law' of the stars, or their mathematical positions) reality.

Astrology as a calendar follows the Earth's seasons and cycles, not the literal stars. You have to remember that those who discovered astrology were exceptional mathematicians, and were able to calculate the changes in position. One astrologer explains it this way, "Hipparchus and other astronomers knew that, eventually, a different constellation would be Sol's backdrop on the equinox. But that didn't bother them, since the zodiac has always been a symbolic representation of the sky. For thousands of years, the tropical zodiac has reflected the steady rhythm of the seasons, not the slow drift of the constellations."[11]

Astrology functions as a way to track the cycles of the earth and her seasons, just like it says in Genesis 1.[12] Over many millennia, ancient civilizations all over the world have found the movements of the celestial bodies of great significance, and over the years they have developed a

---

11. Mungovan, Grace. n.d. "No, Astrologers Haven't Gotten It Wrong — the Media Has | CHANI." https://www.chani.com/blogs/the-history-of-the-zodiac.

12. "The God said: Let there be lights in the dome of the sky, to separate day from night. Let them mark the seasons, the days, and the years" - Genesis 1:14

language to correspond with these movements. Starting in about the third millennium BCE, astrologers began to document natal charts (which are cast using the birthdate, time, and place a person was born), as well as the charts of great astronomical events in order to understand various aspects of a person's personality or to gain clearer knowledge of the future. While these charts did get predictive (especially when used by pagan cultures) they can also be used without attempting to tell the future. Think about how a weather forecast gives us important but general information that is extremely useful (ie. in the northern hemisphere it's probably going to be warmer in July and colder in December). Obviously, we don't think looking at the weather forecast is evil, nor do we fault farmers and gardeners for relying on the Almanac to guide them in their planting and growing. Likewise, modern proponents of Astrology would consider it a helpful tool for navigating life on earth, too- but a poor one for making specific predictions.[13]

One issue with Astrology is that in the past, assertions were made that the planets have power over us, over our future, and specifically over our will. Catholic supporters of astrology like Thomas Aquinas spoke out against this ("the heavenly bodies are not the cause of our willing and choosing").[14] This is no longer the belief-system of most

---

13. Renowned Mundane Astrologer C.E.O. Carter himself said, *"If we look into the past we shall have no reason to congratulate ourselves upon our achievements in this field... When we look for good work in the wider and far more intricate task of mundane astrology, we shall find a few lucky hits and many blunders."* Admitting astrology's weakness in accurately making predictions. Green, H. S., Charles E. O. Carter, and Raphael. 2004. *Mundane Astrology: The Astrology of Nations and States*. Astrology Classics, 213.
14. Aquinas, Saint Thomas. 2014. *The Summa Contra Gentiles*. Aeterna Press, Book 3, LXXXV.

modern astrologers. Still, the fear of overstepping causes many to shy away from any engagement with the subject.

However, just because a tool has been misused does not mean it is useless. The Magi's inclusion in the Gospel story showing that Astrology has been used to guide God's children to Christ is what leads to the plausibility of the assertion that the heavenly bodies, as stated in the Psalms, "declare the glory of God", and create the report that "goes forth through all the earth, their messages, to the ends of the world." *(*Psalm 19:5).

THEOLOGICAL SUPPORT FOR ASTROLOGY

Astrology has been a part of the Christian Church for a long time. Still today, the date for Easter is chosen based on the first Sunday after the full moon on or after the spring equinox.[15] The building for St. Peter's Basilica itself was begun on the carefully selected date and time selected by the astrologers of Pope Julius II.[16] St. Hildegard of Bingen,

---

15. Catholic Answers. n.d. "How Are the Dates for Easter, Palm Sunday, and Ash Wednesday Determined?" https://www.catholic.com/qa/how-is-easter-sunday-determined-palm-sunday-ash-wednesday.

16. "The astrologers of Pope Julius II established that the horoscope of April 18, 1506, at 10:00 a.m. correlated with both the horoscope for the presumed birth of the world and the birth horoscope of Christ. In addition, the locations on the horoscope chart of the Sun, Venus, and Mercury indicated benevolence, while that of Saturn and Mars suggested power and longevity. Jupiter's location was propitious as well, promising wealth. Julius and his Renaissance architects believed that the concordance of the heavens and the radiation emanating from the cosmos provided protection for this building at the time of its founding and, in turn, the building would continue to radiate these powers upon the people associated with it for centuries." Harris, Molly. 2013. "The Horoscope of St. Peter's." National Endowment for the Humanities. https://www.neh.gov/divisions/research/featured-project/the-horoscope-st-peter%E2%80%99s.

Doctor of the Church, discusses celestial events and their meanings in great detail in her Medical text, *Cause et Cure*.[17] Other doctors of the Church, such as St. Thomas Aquinas and St. Albert the Great also make cases for natural astrology in their work, such as this quote by Aquinas in Summa Contra Gentiles:

> "Now the disposition of the human body is subject to the heavenly movements. For Augustine says it is not altogether absurd to ascribe the mere differences between bodies to the influence of the stars: and Damascene says that the various planets produce in us various temperaments, habits, and dispositions. Consequently the heavenly bodies cooperate indirectly to the goodness of our intelligence..."[18]

He goes on to explain that just because our bodies might be influenced by heavenly movement, our intellect and will are not subject to them, because something of a higher order cannot be subject to a lower intelligence. Likewise-astrologer, scientist, and magician St. Albert the Great (who was Aquinas' teacher) felt the same way. Georgetown Professor of History, David J. Collins, S.J. writes, "Albert distinguished the *science of the stars* from anything diabolical, which (he) repeatedly condemned."[19] It is well known that many medieval and renaissance Popes had astrologers, art was created according to astrological signs, and astrology was considered critical to the practice of medicine in

---

17. Berger, Margaret. 1999. *Hildegard of Bingen: On Natural Philosophy and Medicine*. D. S. Brewer.
18. Aquinas, Saint Thomas. 2014. *The Summa Contra Gentiles*. Aeterna Press, Book 3, LXXXIV.
19. Collins, 15.

Medieval times and beyond.[20] Indeed, for much of Christian history, astrology was simply another gift given to the people of Earth by God- albeit misused by many.

Because Astrology was a very common practice in Medieval and Renaissance Europe, it is not surprising that the theologians of the day supported it. The fact of the matter is, theologians have believed things that were found not be true after being subjected to the rigors of academic investigation, and the Church has condemned more than one scientist whose findings went against what was considered sacred doctrine at any given time (here's lookin' at you, Galileo). So let's go back even further into the annals of history to strengthen this case. Here I will rely heavily on the work of Nicholas Campion, a Historian of Astrology and a lecturer at the University of Wales

BUT FIRST.

Before I go back into prehistory I must ensure that the reader and I have an understanding. Since the 'enlightenment', when western society chose to abandon a healthy respect for and recourse to intuition, spirituality, and things unseen in order to fully embrace scientism, we tend to be extremely egotistical when looking at the beliefs and practices of our ancestors. In the words of Campion, "If anatomically modern human beings were alive 80,000 years ago, that rather suggests that they were psychologically modern as well... The whole notion of "primitive" as a moral or intellectual condition needs to be

---

20. Quinlan-McGrath, Mary. 2013. *Influences: Art, Optics, and Astrology in the Italian Renaissance*. The University of Chicago Press.

well and truly abandoned."[21] As I describe the artifacts left behind by those who came before us, I encourage you to not to be tempted to write off our ancestor's discoveries as "primitive" (which may lead you to dismiss the wisdom that these cultures contained). We have much to learn from our elders.

When we look to the past, there is *much* evidence for the use of Astrology- across various cultures, eras, and regions.

A BRIEF HISTORICAL EXAMINATION OF ASTROLOGY

Some of the oldest concrete evidence for the beginnings of modern day astrology can be found in the cave paintings of Lascaux in France, from 15,000 BCE.

"Just above the neck of the largest of the aurochs (the now-extinct bulls), which has a length of 5.5m, are six spots. These are very likely the six most visible stars of the Pleiades, the star cluster which tradition later attached to the shoulder of Taurus, the bull, while further dots on the bull's face may be the Hyades, another star cluster now included in Taurus... The Lascaux paintings offer our clearest evidence yet of a Paleolithic astral religion and a solar calendar as well as the earliest visual evidence for the existence of a zodiacal constellation."[22] [23]

---

21. Campion, Nicholas. 2009. *A History of Western Astrology Volume I: The Ancient World*. Continuum, 4.
22. Campion, 11.
23. "Lascaux Cave." n.d. https://archeologie.culture.gouv.fr/lascaux/en.

Campion continues discussing the Pleiades, "There is a remarkable similarity between stories about them found as far apart as North America, Europe and Australia. All these accounts link the Pleiades to myths of seven sisters (though occasionally brothers) and explain the fact that, often, only six are easily visible with stories to explain how one disappeared or fell to the Earth."[24]

Another example of astrological similarities across the world exists between Ancient Celtic and Indian culture. "A gloss on an 8th Century CE Irish manuscript held in Wurzburg in which the Irish word budh was glossed in Latin." This word represented the planet Mercury, which for the Celts meant 'gift of teaching'. "On the basis that the first wave of written Irish texts represent much earlier oral wisdom, we can assume that Mercury was already 'budh' in the first millennium BCE; in Sanskrit budh means 'to know', or 'to enlighten'. In early versions of The Vedas as well as in modern Indian astrology, the planet Mercury is also known as budh." The fact that the planet Mercury possessed the associations with knowledge and teaching in both Ancient Celtic and Indian culture is

---

24. Campion, 11.

particularly interesting when one considers that these associations are still present in modern astrology.[25]

It is not outside of the realm of possibility that Irish Druids and the astrological systems of the Far East had connected somehow. Much of what we know about the Ancient Druids was handed down to us by Julius Caesar. The Roman Empire- the epicenter of the known world at that time- became a key hub for travelers journeying from distant regions. The idea that someone (or a body of knowledge) from India may have gone as far as the northernmost reaches of the Roman Empire (and shared knowledge and information in the process), or vice versa, is not absurd to imagine. In *The Conquest of Gaul* written in the first century BCE, Julius Caesar shares the fascinating training process of the Druidic Priesthood, which explains why we don't have many records, "although the Druids of Gaul… had developed a system of writing for ordinary record keeping, their 20-year religious training was entirely oral. It was considered that sacred teaching should be committed to memory." Caesar also reported that "The Druids said much about the heavenly bodies and their movements, the size of the universe and of the earth, the physical constitution of the world and the power and properties of the gods."[26]

Unfortunately we have few specifics regarding the cosmology of Northern Europe. We do however have much information regarding the cosmology of Mesopotamia, which is where most of our present understandings of astrology originate. "The earliest evidence of a tradition of astrology as a highly organized

---

25. Campion, 30-31.
26. Campion, 33.

ASTROLOGY

and codified system of reading meaning into the sky emerged in the lowland, lush river valleys of Sumer, which is now Southern Iraq."[27] Astrology became a key aspect of Mesopotamian culture, with its key function being to support its various leaders in preserving stability and order. In fact, the very word "Chaldean" (a semitic people who settled in Babylonia) became synonymous with "astrologer". Alongside the religion of the day, astrology became infused with pagan meaning and practice.

However, polytheism would not be the only religious tradition to emerge out of the fertile lands of the Middle East. Amidst foreign domination and competing ideologies, a distinctive monotheistic belief system would emerge and develop into what we now know as Judaism.

Though distinct, the Jewish people were subject to influence from their pagan neighbors, and the Old Testament is replete with examples of God's chosen people falling prey to superstition. However, they also managed to incorporate many practices in ways that were not contrary to their faith, "By the first century BCE we find the adoption of Babylonian astrological texts to fit Jewish models and later, the incorporation of zodiacs in synagogue design."[28] Perhaps it is out of a tribe that maintained the ancient *magus* practices but still held memory of their Jewish heritage that the Magi came. We may never know. Either way, we do know that there was much mutual influence—over the course of thousands of years—among the people of Mesopotamia and the rest of the known world. This was bound to lead to much knowledge transfer and cultural fusion.

---

27. Campion, 35.
28. Campion, 110.

No one facilitated the knowledge transfer and cultural fusion between Mesopotamia and the rest of the world like the Macedonian King Alexander the Great in the fourth century BCE.

> "His subjugation of Asia up to the borders of Northern India... brought Greek culture into intimate contact with the cultures of Syria, Babylon, Persia and Central Asia, as well as Egypt. The Greek world itself extended from Asia Minor to the Western Mediterranean, to the coasts of France and Spain, and Greek became an international language from Marseilles to the Indus Valley, occupying very much the same position as English in the modern world."[29]

It is not difficult to imagine the "flow of cosmological ideas between Egyptian priests, Babylonian astrologers and Greek philosophers" as a result of these intense cultural encounters. We retain enough historical details from the astrology practiced in this era to recognize that much of what astrologers 'know' about the planets and signs today was knowledge already in use during the centuries before Christ. For example, Babylonian Astrologers knew "that planets might be strong or weak depending on the sign they occupied and that, as in the medieval and modern tradition, Gemini ruled brothers and Taurus was fertile." Christians are not even the first to consider the planets as a form of communication between God to human beings, "If the stars and planets were the writing of the gods and

---

29. Campion, 173.

goddesses to the Babylonians, Plato took the assumption one step further: they were the thoughts of God."[30]

The conquering of the Hellenistic Empire by the Romans explains why astrology retains the use of Roman gods instead of the Greek. This 'changing of the guards' also highlights the tense relationship between astrology and the West. The Greek philosophers had already begun questioning what they considered superstitious practices; and the Stoics, Epicureans, and other elite thinkers leaned away from a literal belief in the pantheon of personalities and toward a belief that religion was useful for social order... but not literally true. Along this same vein, despite being performatively pagan, aspects of Roman society were leaning toward philosophical skepticism and impersonal conceptions of divinity that feel similar to modern secularism. Campion notes that "intellectuals skeptical of the existence of the gods had little time for a science apparently devoted to reading messages from those gods."[31] Remarkably, it is among pagan monuments dedicated to Athena and Zeus, and not within Christian Cathedrals, that astrology is first cast to the fringes of society.

ITS ORIGINS CANNOT BE KNOWN FOR SURE

So what does all of this tell us? Despite the fact that many apologists against astrology claim that it was given to humans by demons (as it states in the book of Enoch), or that it originated with the pagan religions of the Middle East, it seems more likely that "the shamanistic priesthood of the third millennium BCE inherited a system that had

---

30. Campion, 223.
31. Campion, 229.

been evolving over thousands of years."[32] This idea of astrology 'evolving over thousands of years' makes sense when it is positioned as a language and a calendar system.

It would seem absurd to pose the same levels of skepticism and questioning to other languages. Is Chinese scientifically valid? Did demons give us English? When did the Swahili language originate? Can we point to a specific moment in history? The truth is, languages and calendars take time to develop. This 'slow evolution' supports the idea of astrology being created (discovered) through the observation of intelligent people over generations. These people were capable of recognizing patterns, preserving their findings, and they did so for thousands of years—on every single continent. Accordingly, we can well and truly abandon the idea that astrology is the fruit of dumb and desperate humans grasping for meaning in the stars because they didn't know any better, as is sometimes implied.

It is remarkable that various cultures all over the world found significance in the positions of the stars, and not just for seafaring. The stars told stories (gave 'reports', if you will). The practice was only disputed under a 'practically atheist' philosophy—and had fallen out of favor in Rome long before the early church fathers could condemn them (only to be resurrected by medieval Christians a short few hundred years later).[33] Known God-fearing cultures

---

32. Campion, 14.
33. I would be remiss if I did not I mention the robust astrological tradition of the Ancient cultures in the Americas and (notably for those interested in Christian History) the Moors. I say this to remind the reader that astrology was truly a global language, and not confined to Europe, the Middle East, and Asia. North Africa boasted a vast intellectual tradition- not limited to but including groundbreaking medical practices,

embraced astrology, and their respective cosmological traditions grew with the cultural fusion facilitated by the expansion of empires.

While one may argue that almost every culture also did bad things, such as engaging in pagan religious rituals, war and so on (insinuating that just because everyone did it doesn't mean it was good) one must remember that each culture also created their own systems for medicine, government and other social structures. Each population engaged in (and continues to engage in) good and bad traditions.

Now, we are left with the original question—are these Astrological discoveries part of the sinful pagan practices we repugn (the aforementioned 'bad' or even possibly demonic traditions)? Or is it the 'report that goes forth through all the earth' that can be labeled as 'ancient wisdom' alongside categories of knowledge like herbal medicine, the cultivation of crops, midwifery, architecture and so on?

ANSWERING THE ULTIMATE QUESTION

The fact of the matter is, languages and calendars are not inherently evil. They are tools. And like most tools, they can be used for bad or good. You can use an axe to cut firewood or kill a human. Tools are a-moral.

As an example, it is common sense to recognize that there is a difference between a knife and a guillotine. Many of us

---

systems of government, and yes- astronomy and astrology. The glory days of the Moorish Empire brought a wealth of knowledge to post-Roman Europe. Many argue that it is this knowledge that reawakened Christendom's interest in astrology.

have knives in our home, because knives are useful. We can pretty easily explain to our children why they are dangerous and keep them out of reach, and in doing so we ensure that they do not hurt themselves while we all enjoy the benefits. There are few uses for a guillotine other than to chop off heads and so, we do not keep them around.

When wondering about whether or not Astrology is a tool that deserves to be kept around—like a knife, or discarded—like a guillotine, one might ask a most logical question: "Is there any evidence of a' good' (or, in other words, 'God-approved') use for the tool of astrology?"

With a smile, I joyfully point to the biblical story of the Magi, and their use of Astrology to encounter our Heavenly King.

A resounding *yes*.

5
WHAT WOULD JESUS DO?

When I first began embracing astrology, a part of me was afraid.

Don't get me wrong, the results of listening to the language of God and accepting his influence in my life in this manner were unmistakable. My marriage was steadily improving—we were back on track and would never seriously say the word divorce again. The insights I received after looking at my husband's and daughter's charts (and later more children), which allowed me to improve the ways that I related to them and them to me were transformative and life-changing.

Most importantly, I grew closer to God and my prayer life deepened. This is the true fruit, and what I believe actually changed my life. Like the Magi, astrology just pointed me in the right direction.

But this does not mean that everything became perfect overnight. Amidst all of the chaos of 2020 I would go on to experience three miscarriages before conceiving my second daughter. The pain of losing a child reverberates and leaves a permanent mark on a Mother's soul, no matter their size. We still struggled financially as my husband went to school full-time and I attempted to balance my business with the duties of motherhood.

Probably the greatest blessing though, is how astrology influenced my parenting. When my second daughter arrived I saw in her chart that she had some signs which would make her very different from myself and my eldest daughter. I am so grateful that I had these insights before she became a toddler, before I would experience an exhausting pregnancy with my third daughter, and before I might attempt (as so many parents do) to reprimand what would appear like bad behavior out of my child. The fact that I had seen her Star Map meant that I knew that strength, warrior-like bravery, and an immense amount of energy was just how God made her, not something to be punished away.

Basically, I became a better wife and mother— which is definitively not something the devil could ever do. The fruit spoke for itself.

But, I was still afraid of what my church friends would think. I still experienced doubt… had I been tricked? Had the devil, who is so much more cunning than I, used my ego against me? Was I insane to think that *I* had something to teach the Church?!

Like a Good Catholic Girl I decided to take my questions to my Spiritual Director. I was nervous to share what I had been studying- but I knew keeping it a secret would only be proof of sin. I had to get it out in the open, and I decided to tell him everything.

On the day of our appointment, I nervously walked into Fr. Marco's office. As always, he greeted me warmly. I took a deep breath and reminded myself not to chicken out of the scolding I was sure to receive. "The truth does not shy away from questioning," I reminded myself. Deep down, I knew that there is a reason why we need spiritual directors. The soul needs accountability.

No matter what, I would take it on the chin, and I would be obedient—even if he told me never to look at an astrology chart again.

I sat down and quickly told him everything, before I could change my mind.

Miraculously, Fr. Marco did not seem phased. "God is big enough for your questions Janelle", he began slowly—being careful not to give outright approval while still giving me permission to think— "The key here is that you must remain close to God. The devil will try to convince you that God isn't big enough for your questions, that He doesn't care about your curiosities, or that He can't handle your research. That is not true, but you <u>must</u> remain close to God. If you believe there is something here, fine. Look into it, carefully. Just remember that all truth belongs to God, so if you want to learn the truth about any topic you must go to Him. Remain with God and he will not lead you astray."[1] He repeated 'remain with God' many times, as a reminder that seeking was okay, as long as I remained within the safety of the Church.

---

[1]. This is also why I have remained firmly Catholic- regularly praying the rosary, reflecting on the sorrows of Mary daily, and receiving the sacraments. Astrology is not what fills my cup spiritually, it is simply a tool that supports my relationships. No one needs Astrology, *but we all need Jesus Christ*. It is important to keep things in their proper order.

I couldn't believe my ears. Zero condemnation. No insistence that 'the devil was after me'. I was being given permission to think, to ask questions, and to wrestle with God. I breathed a sigh of relief.

Not everyone had seen it that way. I was still in my late 20s, and I think my youth contributed to a certain naiveté in the way that I shared my new knowledge. I simply assumed that people wanted to know the truth. So, I shared my findings sooner than I should have. Word got out that I was exploring the topic, and I got a few well-meaning messages from people who were afraid that I was going down the wrong path. I was happy to share my research with them— but usually they had condemned me to hell before we got too far. Often they would say things like "Astrology is evil", but then they couldn't find the Bible verses to back up their claims (other than the one verse in Isaiah which specifically denounces predictions)[2]. All the other verses and condemnations are against divination, which is not what I was doing.

I told Fr. Marco about the reprimands I had gotten from other Church members. He all but rolled his eyes, "Some see the devil under every rock. You will find what you seek. If you are looking for the devil, you will find him. If you are looking for God, you will find Him. Do not be afraid Janelle, but also- do not go too far." I understood what he meant.

I floated home. *I was allowed to seek.* The Church had room for me and my questions. I wanted everyone to know how

---

2. Isaiah 47:13-14

big and beautiful this Church is, and that it is truly Universal.[3]

It still strikes me that despite the robust intellectual tradition of the Church, some of its members were still resorting to self-imposed ignorance and "because I said so" subjugation tactics. God is a good God, and He is not trying to trick us. He gives ample evidence to support His claims[4], even those which we are called to believe by faith.[5] Just like any good father would not give a child a snake when they ask for bread[6], neither will our God give us confusion and half-truths when we ask for the whole truth.

On the other hand, He will also not lead us into sin, either. The pagan rituals and folklore that were still very real during the time of Christ and after probably meant that the astrology of the day *was* a dangerous practice. It makes sense that the Church, and its Early Fathers, would wholeheartedly condemn it.

But we are living in different times. We know now that planets are just rocks in the sky—not mystical beings, angels or gods. We can laugh at the idea of Jupiter making anyone do anything. We can distance the language from the characters—characters who were only too real during the ancient Roman Empire. We can actually predict the weather now, and be grateful for the ways general weather, political or economic forecasts support our lives without

---

3. The word "Catholic" comes from the Greek *katholikós*, which literally means "universal" or "according to the whole".
4. Barillas, Martin. 2024. "Nuclear Engineer Says Latest Research Confirms First-Century Date of Shroud of Turin – EWTN Great Britain." EWTN. https://ewtn.co.uk/article-nuclear-engineer-says-latest-research-confirms-first-century-date-of-shroud-of-turin/.
5. John 20:29: "Blessed are those who have believed without seeing."
6. Luke 11:11

engaging in fortune telling or divination. This doesn't make us smarter or more evolved than our ancestors—it just means that God has *actually* enlightened us (not to be confused with the faux attempts at enlightenment, by the likes of Machiavelli, Hobbes and Rousseau).

Now that I was more aware of various topics which were embraced by New Age spirituality and denied by Christianity, I started seeing how prejudiced Christians can be against those who consider themselves more spiritual. I realized that Christians often act more like Pharisees than like Jesus.

I decided to look at the gospels and see how Jesus treated the pagans who were earnestly seeking him. What was Christ's response to honest questioning and good faith inquiry?

What I found was more beautiful than I could have imagined.

THE FAITH THAT JESUS PRAISED

Did you know that there are only *two* people whose faith Jesus praised in the gospels?

When I first read about this, I ran over to my Bible to dig into those passages. Two *very* blessed people had their faith PRAISED by Jesus Christ himself, and then those praises were recorded for all Christians across the world to read again and again. What an immense blessing.

It is easy to assume that they must have been people who were close to Christ, like the apostles. Or perhaps that they were devout followers of Judaism, like the people that Jesus grew up with.

But it was neither. Both were pagans.

Before I dive further into who these people were, it is important to note that there were several biblical characters whose faith Christ acknowledged as the 'reason' for their healing or salvation. As an example, there was the woman who had a hemorrhage and whose story is told in Matthew 9, Mark 5, and Luke 8- when she touched Jesus' garment, she was healed. Jesus told her, "Daughter, your faith has healed you. Go in peace and be freed from your suffering."[7] While this is an acknowledgement of her faith —it is not direct praise—so I did not include these biblical characters in this analysis, but only those who received a direct compliment regarding their faith from God.

The first to receive a direct compliment from Christ about his faith was the Roman Centurion, whose story is found in both Matthew 8 and Luke 7.

The two gospels tell the story a bit differently, but I tend to prefer Matthew's retelling. In this gospel, the Roman Centurion approaches Christ for the purpose of interceding—not for himself, and not even for a member of his family—but for a servant. (I think this is so beautiful) Matthew 8, verses 5-10 say:

"When he entered Capernaum, a centurion approached him and appealed to him, saying, 'Lord, my servant is lying at home paralyzed, suffering dreadfully.' He said to him, 'I will come and cure him.' The centurion said in reply, **'Lord, I am not worthy to have you enter under my roof; only say the word and my servant will be healed.** For I also am a person subject to authority, with soldiers subject to me. And I say to one, 'Go,' and he goes;

---

7. Mark 5:34

and to another, 'Come here,' and he comes; and to my slave, 'Do this,' and he does it.' When Jesus heard this, he was amazed and said to those following him, 'Amen, I say to you, in no one in Israel have I found such faith.'"

Imagine, *amazing* Jesus! The centurion's words have resonated so profoundly across time that those of us who celebrate the Latin Rites of the mass still repeat his words aloud during the liturgy.

In Roman times, Centurions were expected to participate in state religious rituals, which included offerings to the Roman gods and emperor worship. Complete submission to the Emperor and Roman customs were required. Refusing to submit could be seen as disloyalty or treason. While Jews were conscripted into the army, they would have a difficult time reaching the higher ranks without abandoning their Jewish traditions. Those who we read in history who did ascend to these higher military ranks were typically Jewish by name or by descent only (much like the phenomenon of cultural Judaism we witness today).[8] Because of this, we can safely assume the Centurion was a pagan. However, he was known for being kind to the Jewish people.[9]

Regardless, he was clearly someone who recognized God when he saw him, much like the Magi. Jesus gave him a great compliment for it, and the Catholic Church has immortalized his words, ever since.

The second person to be complimented for their faith was

---

8. Roth, Jonathan. n.d. Review of *Review of: Military Service and the Integration of Jews into the Roman Empire*, by Raúl González-Salinero. *Bryn Mawr Classical Review*.
9. In the Luke 7: 1-10 version of the story, the Jewish elders said to Jesus "he loves our nation and he built the synagogue for us."

a Canaanite woman. We find her story in Matthew 15: 21-28:

"Then Jesus went from that place and withdrew to the region of Tyre and Sidon. And behold, a Canaanite woman of that district came and called out, 'Have pity on me, Lord, Son of David! My daughter is tormented by a demon.' But he did not say a word in answer to her. His disciples came and asked him, 'Send her away, for she keeps calling out after us.' He said in reply, 'I was sent only to the lost sheep of the house of Israel.' But the woman came and did him homage, saying, 'Lord, help me.' He said in reply, 'It is not right to take the food of the children and throw it to the dogs.' She said, 'Please, Lord, for even the dogs eat the scraps that fall from the table of their masters.' Then Jesus said to her in reply, 'O woman, great is your faith! Let it be done for you as you wish.' And her daughter was healed from that hour."[10]

"O woman, great is your faith." Wow.

Here we have two people, a man and a woman. Both pagans, one pagan for sure. Both interceding not for their own healing, but for the healing of another. Both distinctly praised by Christ.

Sandra Schneiders, a nun and professor of theology at the Jesuit School of Theology in Berkeley says the following about these stories,

> "In the New Testament faith is not presented as a univocal notion. Jesus praised the faith of people

---

10. While Jesus' response may seem harsh—He was making the point that He was operating at that time and place specifically for the Jews of that city. It was her insistence in faith that led to Him honoring her request.

who not only did not know who he was... but who did not share the monotheistic belief of Israel... In one case he said of a pagan, 'Truly I tell you, in no one in Israel have I found such faith' (Matt. 8:10) In another, he granted the petition of a Syrophoenician woman, saying to her, 'O woman, great is your faith!' (Matt. 15:28). Faith, then, is not exclusively adherence to a revealed law. What it seems to mean in such cases is a fundamental openness of the person to transcendence. **What people whose faith has saved them seem to have in common was their resistance to the primordial human temptation to make oneself the measure of the possible**. These people were willing to accept the possibility that something could exist, could act, that went beyond their own knowledge and powers. They were willing to appeal for help and to accept it from a source they did not understand or control."[11]

Speaking for myself, I have fallen short of this 'fundamental openness to transcendence' many times. So often—in particular when I do not remain in prayer—my ego takes over, thinking I'm in charge. I want things to go my way, I want to please my desires, and I want success based on my demands. I often forget to humble myself before the Lord, and to submit (literally 'to place under') myself to His Kingship and sovereignty. I have much to learn from these New Testament examples of faith and humility. I'm sure most of us do.

---

11. Schneiders, Sandra. 1999. *The Revelatory Text: Interpreting the New Testament as Sacred Scripture, Second Edition.* The Liturgical Press. 59-60.

WHAT WOULD JESUS DO?

I DID NOT COME TO JUDGE THE WORLD, BUT TO SAVE THE WORLD

[12]Before he died, the late Pope Francis caught a lot of flack for saying that "all religions are paths to God." Many Catholics and Christians online tore that phrase apart, saying that he was advocating for universalism, pantheism, and some even said that the Holy Father was a heretic.

It is important to acknowledge what Pope Francis did not say.[13] Pope Francis did not say that all religions are paths to salvation. Salvation only comes through Jesus Christ, but all religions in some way are seeking transcendence, and that the willingness to seek something above and outside of yourself is the search for God. Pope Francis was advocating for healthy inter-religious dialogue, where the conversation can start with something like, "I can see that through your religious practice you are seeking God" rather than, "all your gods are demons and you are going to hell." The difference between those two conversations is obvious, and in light of the faith that Jesus praised in the Gospels—the first statement is likely the truer (and the closest to what Christ himself would have said) of the two.[14]

Now, as with Pope Francis, please note what I am not saying. I am not saying other religions are more true, or more correct than Christianity. I am also not saying that

---

12. John 12:47
13. Fire & Fiat: Embracing Faith with Matt & Shannon, dir. 2024. *Are All Religions Paths to God? Pope Francis Was Completely in Line with Catholic Teaching.* 03:40. https://www.youtube.com/watch?v=lLc9QDS5C2s.
14. The Vatican II document, Nostra Aetate, dives much deeper into the Catholic Church's official position on interreligious dialogue, in case you want to take a closer look.

salvation exists outside of Jesus Christ. Finally, I am not saying that Astrology is somehow necessary for salvation. Of course not! Simply, we do not understand the ways of God, and we shouldn't pretend to.

Before we point the finger at others or pride ourselves with the 'correctness' of our faith (and certainly, before we condemn others to hell...) let's ensure that we are exemplifying a faith that Jesus would praise—a faith that is humble, open to correction, and that is in the service of others.

Unfortunately, the 'Church pop-culture' has not been exemplifying this humble approach to God and one another lately, especially online. Let's take a closer look at how sensationalism, social media, and 'virality' have impacted the Church online.

6

"EVERYTHING IS DEMONIC"

A COMMENTARY ON THE CULTURAL RESPONSE TO SPIRITUALITY WITHIN THE CHURCH

I will never forget a sermon I heard while I was at the very beginning stages of exploring astrology. It was Christmas 2020, and since the Churches were closed we were watching mass on TV. Fr. Ripperger (a well-known priest exorcist who claims to talk to demons...) was preaching on the Magi, and made gross misinterpretations. "The Magi were astrologers, yes, but they were sinful." he said confidently, "It was their evil astrological predictions that led them to Jerusalem instead of Bethlehem, and that's why the infants were murdered! Because they weren't being led by God, but by a demon!" I looked around, incredulous, as my well-meaning parents nodded along. They were worried about my recent interest, and I think they hoped that I would be inspired by the 'message' I was hearing. Later, I had gone back to the Bible to review the passage— "A demon?" I asked myself, "Is that even in here?" It wasn't.

"The gifts are further proof of their magic!" he continued, while I wondered what version of the Bible he was using.

"Those gifts—gold, frankincense and myrrh—they were the ingredients they used in their evil divinations! But they laid them down at the feet of Jesus to show that they were giving up the dark arts forever." I did my best to hold back a chuckle. Frankincense... which even today is known as the "king of essential oils", is renowned for its healing properties, and which was sitting on my mothers shelf as we listened—that was a tool for evil? Gold—which God rewarded King Solomon with in spades (to the point where silver basically became useless because of the sheer abundance of precious metals)[1]. Myrrh—one of the most important oils in the Old Testament, featured no less than <u>eleven</u> times and which was one of the anointing oils with which the tabernacle was prepared...[2] those were the evil tools of divination?

He wasn't done- "When it says they 'went home another way', it means that they abandoned their old practices to follow Christ. And they never practiced astrology or magic again" the priest ended proudly, convinced that he had just made a case against astrology... despite not using a single fact to support his argument. I felt embarrassed for him and lamented that Churches closing meant that we were confined to these types of superstitious sermons. "Someone should give him a Bible for Christmas", I muttered under my breath.

My sweet parents looked at me, convinced this was an answer to prayer, "Janelle— I think you heard an important message today!" I wondered how many other young adults and teenagers had been forced to listen to this

---

1. 1 Kings 10:21
2. "Myrrh." 2008. Jewish Virtual Library. https://www.jewishvirtuallibrary.org/myrrh.

message, and received the same side glances and well-meaning comments. I wondered how many of them had been convinced. I certainly wasn't.

Shortly thereafter, I received another message from a woman who was a very recent convert. She sent me a list of what an exorcist supposedly said were portals to the demonic. "I'm just worried about you" she wrote, "I thought you ought to see this". When I read the list, I face-palmed. Of course, there were all of the normal things—like tarot, ouija boards, seances, and the like. But the list also included Alex and Ani bracelets, Harry Potter, massage, and essential oils (yes... the same oils mentioned in the books of Exodus, Song of Songs, Matthew... and of course, the story of the Magi). Astrology was also on the list. *Sigh*.

THE CHURCH INTELLIGENT VERSUS THE CHURCH INDOLENT

In *The Vocation of the Theologian* by Mary Ann Donovan, she discusses a Dogmatic Constitution of the Church, *Lumen Gentium*, noting, "It restored a patristic notion of the Church as mysterion, teaching that 'the Church, in Christ, is a sacrament— a sign and instrument, that is, of communion with God and of the unity of the entire human race" (no. I)."[3] I have thought deeply regarding the unity of the entire human race and the ways in which we approach the various cultural practices found in each section of our world. While the Church Magisterium (at least in recent years) implores us repeatedly to be open to discussion and kind when encountering non-Christian

---

3. Donovan, Mary Ann. 2004. "The Vocation of the Theologian." *Theological Studies* 65 (1), 6.

cultural practices and customs, unfortunately, American-Catholic/Christian-Pop-Culture online remains rigid and heavily focused on condemnation.

My personal approach seems to be in line with Lutheran Theologian Paul Tillich's philosophy—to promote a theology of *"synthesis"*—or the interrelation of Christianity with cultural and societal philosophies.[4] Rather than maintaining a posture of 'us' and the 'other', how can we find common ground, and maintain important differences while still acknowledging the validity of both?

THE EVIDENCE IS CLEAR

The fact of the matter is, interest in ancient spiritual traditions has experienced a resurgence in recent decades, and no level of fear-mongering, demonology or "you're going to hell" is going to convince intelligent people that scheduling a normal massage will invite in demons. While we *absolutely are* in a very real spiritual battle (a fact I will never make light of or pretend isn't true), it is widely and wrongly held within Church culture (not Church Dogma, to be clear) that *any* practice which is not Judeo-Christian in origin—such as Eastern practices that have their roots in foreign spiritual traditions- are evil and are exclusively

---

4. Kennedy, Philip. 2010. *Twentieth-Century Theologians: A New Introduction to Modern Christian Thought*. I.B. Tauris, ch. 8.

portals to the demonic.[5] [6] [7] This is a categorical error that puts Christians at risk of fanaticism.

The physical sciences are beginning to challenge such misleading and frankly, euro-centric belief systems. Much of the Eastern Ancient Spiritual Tradition is based upon the belief that within every living thing there is an energetic or spiritual life force flowing within, known as "Qi" (Chi) or "Prana".[8,9] Modern Quantum Physics, though it wouldn't use this language, does support the idea. The 'building blocks' that make up every single thing in the known Universe, is actually a subatomic phenomenon made up of kinetic and potential energy, called quarks.[10] This energy is present within the substantial "empty" (as we used to think) space inside of atoms, which is not actually empty at all.[11] Furthermore, through the well-known Double-Slit Experiment, Physics shows that an observer can affect electrons without touching them, and

---

5. Ripperger, Chad, dir. 2024 *The Most Common Way Demons Sneak Into People's Lives — Fr. Ripperger - YouTube*. https://www.youtube.com/watch?v=6Rg5e4N8o6c.
6. Michael Knowles, dir. 2022. *Former Astrologist Explains Danger of New Age Practices | Angelamarie Scafidi*. https://www.youtube.com/watch?v=HRxWGRocxYg.
7. Pacwa, Mitch. 1992. *Catholics and the New Age*. Servant.
8. Moy, Tsao-Lin E. 2025. "An Introduction To Chi Energy: Signs Of Imbalance + How To Get Back On Track." Mindbodygreen, August 7. https://www.mindbodygreen.com/articles/what-is-chi.
9. Manasa, B, Srikanth N. Jois, and K Nagendra Prasad. "Prana – The Vital Energy in Different Cultures: Review on Knowledge and Practice." *Journal of Natural Remedies* 20, no. 3 (2020): 128–39. https://doi.org/10.18311/jnr/2020/24487.
10. Lincoln, Don. "Each of Our Bodies Is Proof of Einstein's Equation." *Big Think*, April 16, 2023. https://bigthink.com/hard-science/your-body-energy-field-proof-einstein-equation/.
11. Leinweber, Derek. "Visualizations of Quantum Chromodynamics," 2004. http://www.physics.adelaide.edu.au/theory/staff/leinweber/VisualQCD/Nobel/index.html.

change their behavior through mere intention.[12,13] This has the possibility of challenging some of our beliefs regarding the connectivity of ourselves, and our consciousness, to the world around us. Dr. Ethan Siegel, Astrophysicist, said of the experiments, "What's going on here? It's as though the electrons "know" whether you're watching them or not. The very act of observing this setup—of asking 'Which slit did each electron pass through?'—changes the outcome of the experiment."[14]

An Ancient Chinese book of Medicine (from about 300 BCE), *The Yellow Emperor's Classic of Medicine* shows that mankind has known and taught ways to maintain health and vitality for centuries- long before modern medicine.

> "These days, people have changed their way of life. They drink wine as though it were water, indulge excessively in destructive activities, drain their jing– the body's essence that is stored in the kidneys– and deplete their qi... Seeking emotional excitement and momentary pleasures, people disregard the natural rhythm and order of the universe."[15]

This sound advice confirms the fact that intelligent human beings existed in every society, even without modern science. Again, the Catechism of the Catholic Church tells

---

12. Siegel, Ethan. "Measuring Reality Really Does Affect What You Observe." *Big Think*, April 13, 2023. https://bigthink.com/starts-with-a-bang/measuring-reality-affect-observe/.
13. Fedoseev, Vitaly, Hanzhen Lin, Yu-Kun Lu, Yoo Kyung Lee, Jiahao Lyu, and Wolfgang Ketterle. "Coherent and Incoherent Light Scattering by Single-Atom Wave Packets." *Physical Review Letters* 135, no. 4 (2025): 043601. https://doi.org/10.1103/zwhd-1k2t.
14. Siegel, "Measuring Reality".
15. Ni, Maoshing. 1995. *The Yellow Emperor's Classic of Medicine: A New Translation of the Neijing Suwen with Commentary*. Shambhala.

us, "at every time and in every place, God draws close to man."[16] Our elders have wisdom to share with us. God was speaking to them too. We would do well to humble ourselves and be willing to learn, rather than to automatically judge belief systems that originate with ideologies different than our own.

THE DIFFERENCE BETWEEN THE CHURCH MAGISTERIUM'S RESPONSE TO ANCIENT SPIRITUAL PRACTICES, AND THAT OF POPULAR CATHOLIC CULTURE

Over the past 40 years, the Roman Catholic Church Magisterium and the Roman Catholic Laity have responded quite differently to what is called the 'New Age' phenomenon. We will start by discussing the Church's official response, which is exceptionally measured and rational.

In 1989 the Vatican published a document which mentions the New Age, specifically discussing meditation and prayer. In this document they state,

> "With the present diffusion of eastern methods of meditation in the Christian world and in ecclesial communities, we find ourselves faced with a pointed renewal of an attempt, which is not free from dangers and errors, to fuse Christian meditation with that which is non-Christian."[17]

---

16. Ratzinger, Joseph Cardinal. *Catechism of the Catholic Church.* Image, Doubleday, 1995, 1.
17. "Letter to the Bishops of the Catholic Church on Some Aspects of Christian Meditation – Orationis Formas," 1989, 12. https://www.

In the footnotes of the same document, Pope Saint John Paul II is quoted in a homily given on November 1st, 1982 "Any method of prayer is valid insofar as it is inspired by Christ and leads to Christ who is the Way, the Truth and the Life (cf. Jn 14:6)." It is clearly stated in this document that the problem is not with the practice of meditation itself (notice the the phrase "Christian Meditation" is used), but rather the fusion, of meditation and prayer with un-Christian beliefs and/or heretical ideology. Of course, any Christian educated in the mystical tradition of our faith knows that Christians have practiced various forms of meditation and contemplation from the beginning. Even Eastern strands of Catholicism, such as the Chaldean or Byzantine Rights maintain their Eastern liturgies.

However, there are valid arguments against adopting Eastern spiritual beliefs blindly. In 1996, Joseph Cardinal Ratzinger, who later became Pope Benedict XVI, wrote 'The Current Situation of Faith and Theology' when meeting with the Doctrinal Commissions of Latin America. Here, he also discussed the dangers of what he called "New Age" ideology. For the new age supporter, "The Absolute is not to be believed, but to be experienced. God is not a person to be distinguished from the world, but a spiritual energy present in the universe... This is not only renouncing modernity but man himself."[18] Indeed, the reduction of God from our absolute, omnipotent and ever-present creator (as the catechism says, "the beginning and

---

vatican.va/roman_curia/congregations/cfaith/documents/rc_con_cfaith_doc_19891015_meditazione-cristiana_en.html.
18. Ratzinger, Joseph. "The Current Situation of Faith and Theology -," 1996, 6. https://www.vatican.va/roman_curia/congregations/cfaith/incontri/rc_con_cfaith_19960507_guadalajara-ratzinger_en.html.

end of all things"[19]) to simply a spiritual energy present in the Universe is not a small error. Science may have proven that something like "Chi" exists, but it's not God. It is part of and dependent on creation, and God is not. On this point science and theology can meet, and theology can take it from there.

THE DIFFERENCE BETWEEN "ANCIENT SPIRITUAL PRACTICES" AND "NEW AGE" SPIRITUALITY

Theologically, there is a lot wrong with New Age Spirituality. It is gnostic in origin, meaning that our bodies are fundamentally separate from our souls, and that there is 'secret knowledge' we must attempt to discover through ritual and apocryphal texts. New Age spirituality also teaches that all human beings are divine manifestations of God, rather than children made in his image. A main tenant of New Age Spirituality is that we ourselves, along with the rest of creation, are like miniature versions of God.[20] In 2003, the Pontifical Council for Culture and Inter-religious Dialogue released a provisional report entitled, *Jesus Christ: The Bearer of the Water of Life: A Christian reflection on the "New Age"*. It states, "Even if it can be admitted that New Age religiosity in some way responds to the legitimate spiritual longing of human nature, it must be acknowledged that its attempts to do so run counter to Christian revelation."[21] The document also acknowledges,

---

19. United States Catholic Conference, Inc, *Catechism of the Catholic Church*. New York: DOUBLEDAY, 1994, 198.
20. "New Age Movement | Spiritualism, Holistic Health & Mysticism | Britannica.". https://www.britannica.com/topic/New-Age-movement.
21. Pontifical Council for Culture and Interreligious Dialogue. "Jesus Christ The Bearer Of The Water Of Life - A Christian Reflection on the

"It would be unwise and untrue to say that everything connected with the New Age movement is good, or that everything about it is bad."[22] This moderate and calculated approach is fitting with the Church's commitment to investigate and teach the truth without error.

Contrary to this reasonable response, some members of the laity and clergy, including several exorcists who claim to extract information from demons during exorcisms[23], have stated that basically all practices associated with New Age or Eastern Spiritual traditions are demonic and should be avoided categorically. They are using supposed information given to exorcists by demons during exorcisms as their evidence. After doing a deep dive into the testimonies of various exorcists on Youtube, author Charles D. Fraune notes, "Exorcists learn much of what they know from the time they spend interacting with demons within exorcisms. Demons will talk and exorcists have recounted that they can even get the demons to talk to one another during an exorcism."[24] This problematic statement, and its inherent belief system presents an issue. The Church does not recognize information spoken by demons during exorcisms as 'educational material'. In fact, the Church teaches, as Christ himself taught, that demons are liars[25]. In interacting unnecessarily with demons, and then sharing with the public what demons share with

---

New Age," 2003, 1.4. https://www.vatican.va/roman_curia/pontifical_councils/interelg/documents/rc_pc_interelg_doc_20030203_new-age_en.html.
22. "The Water Of Life", 2.
23. Fraune, Charles D. *Slaying Dragons: What Exorcists See and What We Should Know*. 2nd ed. Slaying Dragons Press, 2019, 5.
24. Fraune, *Slaying Dragons*, 5.
25. New American Bible, "... *he (the devil) is a liar and the father of lies*", John 8:44.

them, these exorcists are, by extension, acting as a conduit for demons to educate the laity. This is troubling, at best.

Even more problematic is the momentum such conversations gain on social media. Videos featuring demonic activity and interviews with exorcists tend to gain more traction than religious interviews on other topics. While there is merit to being aware of the demonic and educating ourselves in spiritual warfare, we must question whether these conversations are teaching the truth, or if they are simply offering the dopamine hits we desire from entertainment.

What sensational videos and fear-mongering definitely <u>are not</u>, is the true teaching of Christ's Church, the Magisterium, and the Apostles. It is important that we differentiate between authoritative Church teaching and that of priests, laity and religious leaders who are exaggerating the Magisterium's claims in sensational ways that stir up the masses.

Prominent Theologian Cardinal Avery Dulles has a special name for those who want black and white answers, and who categorically condemn entire realms of knowledge. He refers to them as "anti-intellectual bigots"—which he defines as "non-theologians who want simple and secure answers to every conceivable question".[26]

When discussing these (or any) topic with Catholic and non-Catholics alike, we must remember that we are being judged as members of the faith. Non-sensical arguments based on emotion and desire rather than fact will only contribute to those who claim that religion is just nonsense.

---

26. Dulles, Avery. *The Craft of Theology: From Symbol to System*. Crossroad Publishing, 1995, 160.

We must honor the intellectual tradition of our Church and ensure our claims can be supported by reason whenever possible.

A NOTE FOR THOSE CONCERNED THAT THEIR CHILDREN ARE DABBLING IN THE NEW AGE

As a former teacher and a mother, I feel a responsibility to address this topic. Many are concerned about the lack of religiosity among the youth. Practices like yoga and astrology have become mainstream. A group of girls will walk into a crystal shop like they are shopping at a convenience store. Popular youtube theologians denounce all such practices as demonic and evil—but the kids don't seem to care.

It is important to recognize what constitutes an evil practice, rather than allowing labels to consume you. Evil is attempting to gain power or control over the future, to use another's energy to create a desired outcome, or to summon spirits or the dead (this is not an all-encompassing definition, just one that pertains to the topic at hand). When judging an activity or item—judge it by these terms. Are they using astrology to predict the future, or just to get a better sense of who they are? Are they using yoga to stretch, or are they worshipping Hindu Gods? Are they buying crystals because they are pretty and bring good energy (dare I say chi) into their space, or are they attempting to infuse crystals with some sort of power to create a desired outcome (such as the attention of a romantic partner, for example).

We can all see the difference between these activities. While I do not make light of actual witchcraft, often it is the very children who grow up in hyper-religious households who succumb to darkness, because when everything is demonic, nothing is.

Even the child who plays with a ouija board or tries tarot is looking for something. Perhaps they are seeking connection, security in the future, or something else. Don't get me wrong, these are dangerous activities. But rather than teaching a child to live in fear, ask them what it is they are looking for in those things. Allow it to be the beginning of a conversation, and don't interrupt while they share (it will seriously reduce their trust in you). Gently and with love, explain to them (using logic and reason *alongside* religion) why they are evil— using the definitions above— and give them positive alternatives. Maybe go with them to various crystal shops and teach them how to discern which ones feel good, and which ones feel dark (maybe all of them feel dark compared to religious stores). Help them find religious jewelry with the crystals they desire embedded or incorporated in them. Let them see that you are a grounded, logical person and they will learn that you are someone they can trust. When they trust you, they will listen to you (more, at least).

This methods work best when the children are young. Teach them *how to spot* evil, rather than simply categorically labeling practices as evil, without a logical explanation.

Believe it or not, parents have so much more to fear from sleepovers, screens and social media apps (and dangerous adults or older children within their own social group who pretend to love their children but have other intentions in mind). I am grateful to my parents for rarely letting me sleep over anywhere. Despite their eagerness for me to hear Fr. Ripperger's sermon at the beginning of this chapter, my intelligent parents have come around and are cheering me on in my studies.

I know that if you are reading this, you deeply love your children. With God as your companion you will certainly discern how to raise them well.[27]

---

27. On my youtube channel, I often discuss parenting using your child's astrology chart as a guide. "Mom, Just Look at my Stars" is a great place to start. Feel free to go to https://www.youtube.com/@JanelleMLara to access those resources.

7
WHAT IS THE POINT?

Right before I decided to move forward in writing this book, I once again felt a twinge of doubt. "What if I'm wrong?" I thought, feeling the weight of what it could mean to publicly encourage Christians to use Astrology. "What if they misunderstand me?"

Even though I was 99% sure, I still felt a hint of fear. The truth is, I would rather die than lead anyone astray. Like Gideon, I just needed *one* more sign to confirm the mission.[1]

"Lord," I whispered, while getting in the car to go pray at the Church, "You know how dense I am. If this is truly your mission for me, just make it abundantly clear. Make it so clear that a blind man could see it."

I parked my car in front of our home Parish, hoping that the doors would be unlocked. As I walked up the steps, I once again committed to full obedience. I reminded myself

---

1. Judges 6:36–40

that no matter what, I would trust in God—even if he told me to abandon the project. Gently, I pulled the door open, trying to be quiet in case someone was praying.

Once inside, I looked around and, finding myself alone, let my gaze fall upon the altar.

I gasped. My eyes quickly filled with tears.

There were stars *everywhere.*

It was either the week before or the week after the feast of the Epiphany (Three Kings Day)— and the Church was decorated for the celebration of the Magi—something I had not expected.

These decorations were more lavish than I had ever seen— stars filled the Church, covering the banners, on the pillars, all leading to the one big star that hung above the beautiful Nativity scene featuring the Christ child and, you guessed it—gorgeous statues of the Three Kings as they journeyed toward Christ.

I collapsed into a pew, and sobbed. "I love you, Janelle" I heard God's deep, gentle and caring voice as I thanked Him for his generosity and kindness.

EVERYTHING I CHOSE NOT TO SAY

"But Janelle, what about St. Augustine? What about all of the Early Church Fathers who denounced astrology, and Pope Sylvester II who openly supported astrology? What about the Moors, the Renaissance Church, and the Non-Enlightened Enlightenment?"

It's true, there is much that I chose not to discuss in depth in this book. The fact of the matter is, Augustine saying that all astrologers talk one way *while also* acknowledging that the planets do influence the earth,[2] the fact that during various moments of the Church she has both embraced and repudiated astrology, and the fact that Dante put astrologers in his version of hell *while also* acknowledging that his sun in Gemini is what gave him his genius[3]... all these facts do is confirm that for the last two thousand years, the Church's relationship with astrology has been... *complicated*. Astrology has been like an unfortunate mistress —being sent away at the first call for 'tradition' or accusation of witchcraft, and then sought again and referenced by those who venerated the sciences of the day.

The truth is not so difficult to find. The practice is either valid or it's not, and rather than choosing to focus on the confusion and debate, I have focused on what is true.

THE TRUTH

The truth is as follows: Astrology is a historic practice with evidence as early as 15,000 BCE, and it was practiced in some form or fashion by nearly every culture across the globe.

While it can be used for predictions, it was also used to lead Gentiles to Jesus. We have no reason to believe that the Magi ceased their use of astrology after encountering Christ. Two of the greatest Doctors of the Catholic Church—St. Albert the Great and St. Thomas Aquinas—defended astrology and, in my opinion, outlined the single best position one can hold on the matter (the opinion that

---

2. Augustine of Hippo. 2004. *City of God (Penguin Classics): Augustine of Hippo, Bettenson, Henry*. Penguin Classics, Book V, Ch. 7.
3. Alighieri, Dante. n.d. "The Project Gutenberg eBook of The Divine Comedy, Paradise." https://www.gutenberg.org/files/1003/1003-h/1003-h.htm#CantoIII.XXII, 110-117.

it affects us, but it does not supersede our free will). What is most certain is that astrology does not hold power over the most-high God. In fact, it communicates to us via very real reports that we can and are expected to understand because, literally, "the heavens declare the glory of God".

Finally, being that astrology is a code of communication (a language) and is not necessarily a scientific reality (yet) means that it doesn't need to be supported astronomically or otherwise, even though it may one day be. Just like the concept of Chi was still true before we discovered Quantum Physics, in the future we may understand scientifically the mechanics of this language God has given us—but we don't have to understand it for it to be true.

It is with these facts in mind that I gratefully practice natal and mundane astrology. Of course, I don't attempt to know or predict the future, and I don't allow it to replace my prayer time or humble submission to God's will. I simply use astrology as a tool to support me in my vocation as a Wife, Mother, and most importantly, as a Christian Woman.

IN CONCLUSION

My intention for this book is to support intellectually what so many of us already know intuitively- that creation reveals God to us in so many more ways than we have traditionally been allowed to acknowledge, and that God is attempting to communicate with us in so many more ways than we have been taught to discern.

My belief is that our journey through this life alongside Jesus Christ is designed to be like a journey alongside a very best friend, an adoring parent and a firm teacher all at once. Like the woman at the well, the one lost sheep, or the Magi- our Savior seeks us, finds us, and uses every medium possible to call out to us and draw us to Him. He desperately wants us with Him in Heaven—every last one of us.

It would be wise to keep in mind the Church's true position on what practices we should reject:[4]

"All forms of divination are to be rejected: recourse to Satan or demons, conjuring up the dead or other practices falsely supposed to 'unveil' the future. Consulting horoscopes, astrology, palm reading, interpretation of omens and lots, the phenomena of clairvoyance, and recourse to mediums all conceal a desire for power over time, history, and, in the last analysis, other human beings, as well as a wish to conciliate hidden powers. They contradict the honor, respect, and loving fear that we owe to God alone."[5]

Anything that seeks to 'unveil' the future is forbidden. If you find that you cannot use or practice Astrology without being tempted to gain power over others, then Astrology is not for you.

Much like with any practice, there are different types of

---

[4]. Remember, this is not an infallible dogma of the Church. In keeping with our robust Intellectual Tradition, many aspects of theology are still up for debate and can change through the revelation of additional truth. This is the task of the Theologian- to verify Church teachings, to hold the Church accountable, and to make new discoveries in theology. With that being said, I do not contradict what the Church teaches here, we absolutely must reject all forms of divination, and "recourse to Satan or demons, conjuring up the dead or other practices falsely supposed to 'unveil' the future".

[5]. United States Catholic Conference, Inc, Catechism of the Catholic Church. New York: DOUBLEDAY, 1994, (2116)

astrology. Judicial Astrology, Horoscopic Astrology, and some forms of Mundane Astrology all attempt to use the stars to answer very specific questions, predict the future, and/or gain knowledge over aspects of creation. These are not Christian uses of Astrology. However, Natal Astrology (when a star map is pulled showing the moment you were born) and Mundane Astrology which seeks to cast a general 'weather forecast' or attempt to look backwards (which is what the Magi did—being that they likely traveled after the initial conjunctions which revealed the birth of Christ) seem to be in the clear.

Remember, this case has been an advocacy for truth, not just astrology. Like anyone who is actually seeking the truth, I am open to being wrong.

WHAT ARE THE IMPLICATIONS OF THIS STORY FOR THE CHURCH TODAY?

In the face of so much intercultural communication, the contemporary Church is now faced with an opportunity to revisit the way we approach ancient spiritual traditions, as well as members of other faiths. I encourage us as the Christian Church to take the *true* message of the Magi (that God is consistently and constantly drawing all of us unto himself) and move forward in our own faith journey—as well as in our relationships with others—with an open heart and an open mind.

The message of the story of the Magi speaks primarily to the desired union between God's 'Chosen People' and the rest of us Gentiles, as well as our joint union with God. Aquinas notes, "We should also remember that some Jews, namely, the shepherds, came to Christ; and some gentiles, namely, the Magi: for Christ is the cornerstone who made the two one."⁶ This is a message for the whole world, and a reminder that we are one human family. Ratzinger reminds us that, "The wise men from the east are a new beginning. They represent the journeying of humanity toward Christ…".⁷ In some way, we are all like the Magi.

I do believe there is a model in the biblical story for the way Christians ought to engage in ecumenical and apologetic conversations. First and foremost, there is no coercion. We can find no evidence of the Magi coming to the Christ-child due to fear, sorrow, or remorse. They simply followed the star using their own time-honored traditions, entered the home and, "fell down and worshiped him".⁸ It would seem that encountering the Christ child, by the exact path they followed in order to do so, was enough.

Some (like Fr. Ripperger) say that the fact that they "departed for their country by another way"⁹ would indicate an abandoning of their pagan traditions—but that simply isn't a part of the story.¹⁰ Theologian D. Mark Davis writes, "The audacity of Matthew's story makes the visit of the magi, among other things, an excellent occasion for considering possibilities for evangelism in a time of heightened interest in alternative spirituality."¹¹ The implications of the story for ecumenism (inter-religious dialogue), evangelization, and the allowance for 'multiple paths to Christ' seems evident across time and culture. Tony Maalouf lends a Liberationist hermeneutic to the

---

6. Aquinas, 2-1.
7. Benedict XVI, p. 97.
8. Matthew 2:11, NABRE.
9. Matthew 2:12, NABRE.
10. Brown, p. 167-168.
11. Davis, p. 420.

conversation, and shows how the story makes a case against racism, in particular that which targets Middle Eastern and Arabic populations (top of mind in the present days of the Israel and Gaza conflicts).[12]

I will conclude with Davis' wise words on the topic:

> "The plain reading of this story is that the magi found the Christ by way of a star. With that simple story line, **Matthew makes one declaration clearly and leaves another set of questions unanswered.** The child Jesus is the one who is born king of the Jews. How that kingship is inaugurated and exercised is answered in the next twenty-seven chapters, but this initial story proclaims the message of Jesus as the promised one. What is not answered, either in this story or in the next twenty-seven chapters, is whether the magi, as a result of finding the Christ, forsook their astrology. What is not answered is whether astrology is true, whether it has a "point of contact" with the Christian faith, or whether it is simply the devil's tool of deception. In this sense, Matthew's epiphany story is instructive for the church's call to evangelism. **It raises the possibility that alternative spirituality can be one means of arriving at the Christ, without having to answer the larger questions of the ultimate truth or falsity of alternative spirituality.** What Matthew's story suggests, in what it says and

---

12. Maalouf, Tony T. "The Inclusivity of God's Promises: A Biblical Perspective." *Cultural Encounters* 7, no. 1 (2011), p. 28.

leaves unsaid, is that such penultimate questions might be left at rest in the activity of evangelism."[13]

WHERE DO WE GO FROM HERE?

In the Second Vatican Council document, *Nostra Aetate: Declaration on the Relationship of the Church to Non-Christian Religions* the Catholic Church states,

> "The Church, therefore, urges its sons and daughters to enter with prudence and charity into discussion and collaboration with members of other religions. Let Christians, while witnessing to their own faith and way of life, acknowledge, preserve and encourage the spiritual and moral truths found among non-Christians, together with their social life and culture."[14]

In keeping with the way God chose to draw these Wise Men to himself, this is done without coercion or fear—but rather through love and an innate desire for union with Christ, while also "living at peace with all".[15]

I hope to one day have a larger conversation with Church leaders on this topic, and possibly help draft or influence a document offering specific instructions on how the Church and the laity can handle the introduction and discernment of new or non-western practices. Without minimizing the very real spiritual battle Christian theology teaches that we

---

13. Davis, pgs. 420- 422.
14. Pope Paul VI. "Nostra Aetate: DECLARATION ON THE RELATION OF THE CHURCH TO NON-CHRISTIAN RELIGIONS," October 28, 1965, (2-3).
15. Romans 12:18, NABRE.

face- it is important to acknowledge that the 'spiritual safety' of a practice does not come simply from its 'Western' or Judeo-Christian origins.

The development of an official system of discernment of new (or 'new to us') practices is in order. It stands to reason that Catholics worldwide are going to be confronted with practices that are foreign to Christian tradition on a regular basis. Through this process, the Church can provide an example of how lay Catholics can discern what is right or wrong about the non-western practices they will undoubtedly come across within our globalized culture. It would be supportive for the Catholic Church to give the laity a model by which to discern the wheat from the chaff in Eastern or alternative spiritual traditions- rather than making blanket statements that may reduce trust in the Magisterium and encourage disobedience among the laity.

We need to rely on the truth. I have faith that the Church will get there.

WHY DOES THIS MATTER?

In a more recent conversation with my trusted spiritual director (the same amazing Fr. Marco) I let him know that I was going to start speaking more on astrology. "I just feel God calling me to talk about it more" I said nervously, still programmed as a Good Catholic Girl to expect a reprimand rather than support, "I really want to know what you think."

Once again, I was committed to obedience. If he said no, I would drop it.

He paused for a long time, praying over his response. "Janelle," he began, "there exists freedom to share what you think is important... and this leads to the inherent question. What IS important?" He then posed a thought exercise, "If you knew that you were going to die next week, and your children were old enough to understand, what is the spiritual legacy you would want to leave to them? What is the *one thing* you would make sure they understood before you passed?"

It all snapped into place. "I would want them to know they are deeply loved by their Creator" I began, tears welling up at the thought of my daughters growing up without me, but knowing that if they loved God, they would have all they needed and more. "I would want them to know that they were made for a purpose, and that they are seen, known, and loved. I would want them to know that the Catholic Church is the Church of truth. I would tell them that if they seek God, He will find them and love them, no matter what." I blinked as I wiped my eyes.

"Then focus on that" Fr. Marco said, "This is not about astrology, this is about the Truth." I nodded.

"One last thing, remember that the devil can't *create* anything. He can only use what God has created for his evil purposes. Nothing on earth is inherently evil" he concluded.

NO ONE NEEDS ASTROLOGY, WE ONLY NEED GOD

For my part, I have chosen to acknowledge the truth our ancestors found in the stars, and to allow this ancient tradition to support me in the most important relationships of my life. It works for me.

Maybe you agree with the case I've laid out here, but you

MAGI FROM THE EAST

have no interest in astrology. That is perfectly fine. No one *needs* astrology. *Everyone* needs God.

My hope for all who read this work or who come across me is that they know this—You are seen, known, and loved by a wonderful God who adores you. He created you for a special purpose, and He deeply wants to spend eternity with you. It doesn't matter who you are or where you come from. It doesn't matter what you've done or if you've gone too far in astrology, witchcraft, sexual sin or otherwise. Jesus Christ *loves* you—not with a conditional/Sunday love we've reduced Him to here in the West—nor with an ambivalent love like they preach in the East— but with a deep, abiding, passionate love. A love that knows all of your quirks and talents and vulnerabilities and the things that make you, you. More than that, he created you the way you are—on purpose. Not for you to sin, but so that you can fulfill the urgent and important mission he has set aside for you to fulfill. The mission that is meant to give your life meaning.

I hope you recognize His love, and love Him in return. If you don't know where to go, may I suggest your nearest Catholic Church. The doors are usually open during the day for prayer (especially in the mornings after daily mass). It is usually quiet, sacred, and smells like incense. A divine place to pray.

Go, sit with Him. Let Him love you.

<u>That</u> is the point.

8
(BONUS) ASTROLOGY BASICS

As an Astrologer, I have leveraged my knowledge of the stars to deeply influence my marriage, parenting, relationships with friends and work, and most importantly, my relationship with God.

I truly believe every human being ought to have at least a basic understanding of astrology. It is a language of God. It is the means by which the heavens communicate with us. Astrology is a very potent, and powerful reflection of what is happening here on earth. Every society on Earth has had a version of astrology, which I believe is our Great and Glorious God reaching out to humanity "at every time and in every place."[1]

This 'cliff-notes' guide is by no means exhaustive. In fact, it barely scratches the surface. But hopefully it will be enough to get you started so that you can better understand the 'report that goes forth throughout all the earth".[2]

---

1. Catechism of the Catholic Church, 1.
2. Psalm 19:2-5

In order to make a very complex topic as simple as possible, I want you to think of an astrology chart as a stage or a scene in a book. Every astrology chart is divided into 12 houses, representing 'the setting'. Each of these houses are flavored by a sign—that would determine the weather or emotion of the setting. Then within the houses and signs are planets, asteroids, and mathematical points- you can consider these the 'players' or the actors within the setting. This is how astrology tells a story, reflecting God's will upon the Earth.

Let's get started parsing it out.

THE HOUSES

There are 12 houses, and each one represents a different aspect of your life. The houses are (1) Self, (2) Self-Esteem, Money and Material Possessions, (3) Communication, Childhood, Siblings, and Early Education, (4) Home and Family Life, (5) Children, Creativity and Creation, (6) Everyday Life, Career, and Health, (7) 1:1 Relationships, Friendships, and Partnerships, (8) Sex, Death, Wealth, and Money that isn't yours (such as taxes and inheritances), (9) Religion, Higher Learning and Long-Distance Travel, (10) Your Life Mission, How You Are Seen in the World, and Your Higher Calling, (11) Large Groups of People, Groups of Friends, and Society and (12) Spirituality, Secrets, and God.

1- <u>The House of Self:</u> The first house is cusped by an aspect called your Ascendant. The Ascendant is the first impression you make when people meet you, but they still don't know you very well. Aspects in this house can also determine what you look like. Some would say it is the 'mask' you show to the world. The aspects within the first house reveal quite a bit about yourself, and what you attract to you. I look at the first house to get the clearest picture of what the person experiences and desires on their journey of life. This is one of the directions a person is meant to head toward.

2- <u>The House of Self-Esteem, Money and Material Possessions:</u> The signs and aspects (planets and transits) in the second house show the energy around your self-worth, finances, money that you earn, and the material possessions that you accumulate. It also reflects how you feel about yourself, and how this impacts your place in society. This is a 'success' house.

3- <u>The House of Early Childhood, Communication, and Learning:</u> The third house gives us insight into how you are designed to communicate what you learn. It also reflects early childhood and early education. This is the house of siblings, the neighborhood you grew up in, and short-distance travel.

4- <u>The House of Home and Family:</u> The fourth house is cusped by an aspect called the Imum Coeli (IC) which means '*bottom of the sky*' in Latin. This reflects your most intimate life, your home and family life. It can also reflect your emotions and personal views. We look at the IC to determine what makes someone feel 'at home'. We look to the fourth house to determine how someone wants to experience their home and family life, and how they want to approach the home and family they create. Childhood and one's relationships with their parents can be reflected here as well. How 'at home' did you feel growing up?

5- <u>The House of Creativity and Creation:</u> We look to this house to see what you are called to create, and how you are called to create it. What have you been brought into this world to bring to the world? What do you enjoy creating? This house can also reflect children, child-bearing, because they are part of our co-creations.

6- <u>The House of Everyday Life, Routines, Health and Daily Work:</u> The sixth house reflects your everyday routines and health. It applies to work in the sense that it reflects how we approach our work on a day to day basis. It also reveals what skills and talents come very naturally to you, and can be consulted when asking questions about the health or desired routines of an individual. This is another house of success.

7- <u>The House of Marriage, Intimate Relationships and Partnerships:</u> The seventh house is where we look to find reflections of how you approach one to one relationships. This can be as intimate as marriage, or even friendships and business partnerships and the like. This is the way in which you would like to experience relationships and interact with others on a one-to-one basis. This house is cusped by the 'Descendent', which is directly opposite the 'Ascendant' we discussed in the first house. You will likely choose to marry a partner who reflects attributes similar to the sign of your Descendent.

8- <u>The House of Death, Sex, Taxes, and Inheritances:</u> The eighth house comprises all of those topics that we prefer to keep hidden, or that aren't polite to speak about with company. How deep is someone willing to go? How do they receive money and support that they don't 'earn' themselves? How are they called to build lasting wealth? How are they being called to handle taboo topics such as sex or sometimes scary topics such as death within their life?

(BONUS) ASTROLOGY BASICS

9- <u>The House of God, Religion, Travel and Higher Learning:</u> The ninth house is known as the 'House of God'. This relates to how someone practices religion, relates to God, approaches long-distance travel and culture. If the third house represents Earlier Education, the ninth house represents College and beyond. This is where one's 'area of expertise' might lie.

10- <u>The House of Success and How You are Called to Be Seen in the World:</u> Whatever is in the tenth house will have a major influence on your work and calling in the world. This is a very important house in determining how you are called to be seen on a broad scale, and your Life Mission. It also supports us in determining how you are designed to approach your work. It reflects the highest version of your success, and the larger calling God has placed on your life.

11- <u>The House of Society, Your Larger Community, the Internet, and Humanitarian Interests:</u> This is where you find the energy someone brings to large groups, and how they are called to operate within them (or maybe, as their leader). Not everyone wants to be in the limelight though, and I often look at this house to see whether someone wants to be the star of the show or behind the scenes. Basically, it tells us the role you will play in larger society and your community. Celebrities often have major aspects in this house.

12- <u>The House of Spirituality and Intuition:</u> In Medieval times, this house was known as the house of your enemies. This likely has to do with it being ruled by Neptune, who can often fog and distort your better judgment. However the key with the twelfth house is, whatever is reflected in this house forces you to be in alignment with God. This is the house of spirituality. Not just formal religion and what you think about God, but how you literally relate to God, within your heart of hearts. This also represents your intuition and spiritual gifts. Your connection to your intuition can be found in this house.

SIGNS

The 12 houses determine what we are talking about when we are looking at different aspects of your chart (life). Now the next step, the 12 Zodiac Signs, determine the flavor, or the energy that is present within each house, or 'stage' of your life.

<u>Aries:</u> The energy of Aries is fire. Aries represents passion, new beginnings, leadership, quick decision making, and forward motion. Wherever Aries is in your chart, you can expect to feel a certain level of assertiveness, excitement, and boldness. In its shadow, Aries can be angry or unable to commit, going from one new project to another. Aries also represents your physical body.

<u>Taurus:</u> The energy of Taurus is earth. Taurus represents groundedness, stability, sensuality, beauty, and material comfort. Wherever Taurus is in your chart, you can expect to feel a certain level of stability, security, and a desire for physical beauty and the 'finer things in life'. In its shadow, Taurus can be lazy, stubborn, and unlikely to go out of its comfort zone.

<u>Gemini:</u> The energy of Gemini is air. Gemini represents intellectuality, seeing both perspectives, deep curiosity, and the uncanny ability to teach and communicate what you know. Gemini is all about connection and is often witty, funny, and expressive. In its shadow, Gemini can be flighty, fake, gossipy and inauthentic.

(BONUS) ASTROLOGY BASICS

<u>Cancer:</u> The energy of Cancer is water. Cancer represents motherhood, nurturing, and the home. Wherever Cancer is in your chart, you can expect a lot of maternal energy, deep intuition, the ability to anticipate needs, and deep emotional awareness. In its shadow, Cancer is a martyr figure that can hold a grudge for too long or blames everyone else for its problems.

<u>Leo:</u> The energy of Leo is fire. Leo is the LION! The charismatic leader, the star of the show, the King and Queen. Leo teaches us how to love ourselves, to be willing to be seen, and it is the energy of self-confidence. In its shadow, Leo is self-centered, narcissistic, and can't get over themselves enough to move forward.

<u>Virgo:</u> The energy of Virgo is earth. Virgo represents the standard of perfection, practicality, health, and the desire to do things the *right* way. Virgo represents exceptional executive function. Wherever Virgo is in your chart, you feel an immense amount of pressure to do the right thing. In its shadow, Virgo can be OCD, overly critical, and paralyzed by a fear of failure.

<u>Libra:</u> The energy of Libra is air. Libra is intelligent, relationship-oriented, beautiful, and has an almost compulsive need for balance. Wherever Libra is in your chart, you'll find yourself desiring balance and peace. The scales represent justice. Libra wants everything to be fair. In its shadow, Libra can be a shape-shifter, doing anything to keep the peace or not get in trouble- or conversely, it can become narcissistic and controlling.

<u>Scorpio:</u> The energy of Scorpio is water. Scorpio represents the depths of truth, deep intuition, and all of the forbidden things that we're not 'supposed' to talk about but are fascinated by (think money, sex, and things of the

occult). Wherever Scorpio is in your chart, you want to get to the bottom of things. In its shadow, Scorpio is dishonest, obsessive, and may have an addictive/escapist personality.

Sagittarius: The energy of Sagittarius is fire. Sagittarius represents truth, generosity, adventure, higher education, and a massive appetite for all life has to offer. Wherever Sagittarius is in your chart, you have a desire to master that subject, and become an expert in it. In its shadow, Sagittarius is judgmental, and often flighty and unhinged.

Capricorn: The energy of Capricorn is earth. Capricorn is a natural leader, strategic, and gets the job done. Capricorn represents masculinity, leadership, and business. Think traditional institutions. Wherever Capricorn is in your chart, you can expect a strong desire to stick with tradition and express more discipline. In its shadow, Capricorn is unyielding, demanding, and rigid.

Aquarius: The energy of Aquarius is air. Aquarius represents humanitarian efforts, high intelligence, taking a unique approach to life, and exceptional creativity. Aquarius almost feels like it's from the future. It's very technology oriented. Wherever Aquarius is in your chart, you can expect things to look different from the status quo. In its shadow, Aquarius is unreasonable, weird, and eccentric.

Pisces: The energy of Pisces is water. Pisces represents deep healing gifts, intuition, and an old soul. Wherever Pisces is in your chart you can expect a 'knowing', the ability to connect easily with the divine, and a desire for connection on a spiritual level. In its shadow, Pisces tends towards mental health disorders more than the other signs, and often dissociates from reality, causing delusion.

(BONUS) ASTROLOGY BASICS

THE PLANETS AND SOME MAJOR ASTEROIDS

The Planets are the players within the houses, flavored by the signs. The position of the planets within the houses and signs communicate very specific meaning in a chart. Wherever you find the following planets and asteroids, you will find clarity about some area of your life. For example, your sun is in one of the signs described above—but I'm willing to bet that some reading this will not resonate with their sun sign. If that is the case, I would immediately look at a person's moon and rising signs, or the personal planets, to see if they are somewhere else. That could significantly alter the energy through which someone expresses their personality.

THE PLANETS

<u>Sun</u>: The sun is your umbrella personality. This is how you shine, and it encompasses how you are most likely to show up in the world.

<u>Moon</u>: Your Inner world. This is who you are inside, your heart, in a sense. Some say this is who your truly are. Very few people see this side of you.

<u>Mercury:</u> How you learn and communicate.

Venus: How you love, femininity, and your self-worth. Venus also represents attraction, beauty, and your relationship with women. Venus is known as a benefic, wherever it is, it is usually beneficial.

<u>Mars:</u> Aggression and Passion. How do you take action? How do you go to war, and what will you go to war for? Mars also represents masculinity and your relationship with men.

Jupiter: Expansion, Gifts, and Good Luck. Wherever Jupiter is in your chart, you will experience growth and expansion. Jupiter is known as a benefic—meaning wherever it is, it is usually beneficial.

Saturn: Discipline and Timing. Saturn in your chart shows where you are being reined in and held to a high standard. Saturn also rules consequences. It is known as a malefic, meaning wherever it is in your chart, it is not going to feel great—but ultimately (like everything in your chart), it works for your highest good.

Uranus: Unexpected events, Originality and Innovation. Uranus is where you break from convention and forge your own, more authentic path.

Neptune: Spirituality, Connection to God, and Dreams. Neptune is where you connect to the spiritual world. However, the catch is that delusion can also be present here. You have to be intentional about who and what you are connecting with.

DWARF PLANETS

Pluto: Transformation, Death and Rebirth. Pluto is good luck, but you have to go through hell to get it. Pluto forces you to face the darkness in order to experience all of the blessings life has to offer. It is known as a malefic, meaning wherever it is in your chart, it is not going to feel good- but like everything else, it is working for your highest good.

ASTEROIDS

Chiron: Chiron represents your deepest wounding, and where you have potential for the highest mastery. It is a

(BONUS) ASTROLOGY BASICS

Christ-like energy. Christ was crucified in order to save the world. Every human being too, suffers deeply in order to learn the lessons to help you become all that you were created to be. No human life is void of suffering, though of course its magnitude varies from person to person.

<u>Pallas</u>: The way you think. The strategist—Athena energy. I've heard Pallas described as the 'smart girl'. Wherever Pallas is in your chart, you have insights most people don't have, and superior knowledge inherently.

MATHEMATICAL POINTS

<u>South Node:</u> These are the gifts you came in with. Things you feel comfortable with, even potential addictions or obsessions. Your South Node feels safe, but you are tempted to overindulge because of that.

<u>North Node:</u> The lesson you are meant to learn, God's greater calling on your life. Your north node represents where you need to be pushed out of your comfort zone in order to achieve your highest potential.

Astrology takes years to learn, and I hesitated about including this chapter in the book. But ultimately, I think it will be helpful—even if it gives you a tidbit of insight, or gets you going in the right direction. I highly recommend accessing the "Additional Resources" in this book, and also bringing your questions to prayer.

Of course, I am always available to help. Find me on youtube.com/@JanelleMLara for support.

ADDITIONAL RESOURCES:

As a Christian, attempting to learn about astrology can be intimidating. The truth is, there are few 'safe' places to learn about the practice. The Church has done a fantastic job of completely isolating astrology over the years, making it so that most Astrologers are fully engrossed in New Age Spirituality.

But not all. An *actual* 'new age' is dawning, and I have discovered some incredible resources that maintain God at the center, or at least don't dive too deeply into any spiritual tradition.

FREE RESOURCES:

In general, I highly recommend Naomi Fox Reina and her work at Light-filled Astrology (lightfilledastrology.com). I felt completely safe with her throughout my certification, and she does a great job keeping our "big beautiful God" at the epicenter of everything she teaches. Naomi is a gem.

ADDITIONAL RESOURCES:

You can start by pulling your astrology chart at lightfilled.co/free-charts/

On her website, Naomi offers free foundational courses to help interpret your chart. I recommend taking advantage of those.

Finally, I strive to make my youtube channel: youtube.com/@JanelleMLara a safe and valuable resource for Christians who are interested in exploring Astrology. There I cover topics such as parenting ("Mom, Just Look at my Stars" is a particularly popular video and resource) and relationships. I also review the charts of prominent figures in history, politics, and pop culture. I hope you'll join us!

BEGINNER RESOURCES:

If you would like to dip your toe a bit further into the Basics of Astrology, I highly recommend the book, "Astrology for Beginners: Learn to Read Your Birth Chart" by David Pond. This was a concise, clear and easy to understand guidebook for me as I was just beginning my journey. This book is available on Amazon.

ADVANCED RESOURCES:

If you want to do a deep dive into Astrology to transform your relationships, parenting, and more— again, from a God-centered perspective—then I highly recommend Naomi Fox Reina's Light-filled Astrology Certification. You can type the affiliate link into your browser, or scan the QR code.

https://register.lightfilled.co/lfa-certification-714703?am_id=janelle5976

ADDITIONAL RESOURCES:

May God bless you with wisdom, peace and love as you embark on this journey.

www.ingramcontent.com/pod-product-compliance
Lightning Source LLC
Chambersburg PA
CBHW020909090426
42736CB00008B/552